Also by the author

Having It Your Way
Decisions, Decisions with John Coplans

YOU CAN WIN AT OFFICE POLITICS

Techniques, Tips, and
Step-by-Step Plans for
Coming Out Ahead

Robert Bell, Ph.D.

An Owl Book
Holt, Rinehart and Winston · New York

Most of the persons, corporations, and organizations named in this book are composites from many different sources and therefore do not resemble any one person, corporation, or organization. If a similarity does appear to the reader between one of these fictional persons and entities and a real person and entity, such similarity is coincidental. In a few instances, I have referred to well-known corporations or individuals. These references will be very obvious to the reader because of their importance in the historically significant events under discussion.

The list of bargaining characters in Chapter 49 from *The Art and Science of Negotiation* by Howard Raiffa, Harvard University Press, 1982, is reprinted with the kind permission of the publisher.

Copyright © 1984 by Robert Bell
All rights reserved, including the right to reproduce
this book or portions thereof in any form.
Published by Holt, Rinehart and Winston,
383 Madison Avenue, New York, New York 10017.
Published simultaneously in Canada by Holt,
Rinehart and Winston of Canada, Limited.

Library of Congress Cataloging in Publication Data
Bell, Robert I.
You can win at office politics.
"An Owl book."
Bibliography: p.
Includes index.
1. Office politics. I. Title.
[HF5386.B375 1985]   650.1   85-8494
ISBN: 0-03-005863-5

First published in hardcover by Times Books
in 1984.
First Owl Book Edition—1985
Designed by Doris Borowsky
Printed in the United States of America
10 9 8 7 6 5 4 3 2 1

ISBN 0-03-005863-5

To Rebecca Bell

Acknowledgments

A lot of friends gave me encouragement and advice on this book. In particular, I want to acknowledge the wisdom, generosity, and kindness of Larry Bell, Dingo, Doug Hall, Bobby Higashi, Vahagn Hovannesian, Marek Kanter, Willette Klausner, Ian Masters, Helen McEachrane, Barry Meier, Barry Pascal, Pavel, Sirousse Tabriztchi, and Alan Turner.

I also want to thank Michael Pantaleoni for suggesting I write the book in the first place; Jonathan Dolger, my agent, for enthusiastically staying with it; Ruth Fecych for her superb editorial help; Pamela Lyons for her fine copy editing.

A special thanks to Jonathan Segal and Roger Straus III of Times Books for all of their help, and especially for believing in this book.

TABLE OF CONTENTS

PART II: DUELING

PART III: TRAPPING

PART IV: MUSCLING

PART V: WHISPERING

PART VI: SIDING

PART VII: BARGAINING

YOU CAN WIN AT OFFICE POLITICS

1
An Introduction to Game Theory

IF SOMEBODY AT THE office is pulling a power play on you, and you're not sure what to do about it, you could be in a jam. This book shows how to figure out what to do.

We'll look at situations where you are compelled to make up your mind even though you are torn between alternatives; where you are forced into career duels with colleagues, bosses, and subordinates; where you are caught in a trap, or trying to avoid one; where you are being muscled and may have to muscle back; where you are stuck dealing with what are called office secrets; where you are obliged to take sides when you don't want to; and where, just to live decently, you have to make a deal for a raise, a promotion, or a better job.

This book provides a practical framework for quickly analyzing, deciding, bargaining, and acting. The basis for all the analysis will be Game Theory.

Game Theory

Although the original theory was highly mathematical, many of its subsequent developments have not been, and this book is totally nonmathematical, as a quick flip through the pages will reveal. All of the technical hocus-pocus is skipped, but its implications are put to immediate, practical use. This book distills from Game Theory a method of reasoning that is expressed in a Basic Principle. From this, and in the context of practical applications, twenty-nine corollaries are deduced. Altogether, they constitute a strategic point of view to office politics.

3

This point of view is applied in a series of examples, drawn from actual situations, in which, of course, the names of the individuals and corporations have been changed. The instant you read them, you'll see why this was necessary. These examples aren't stripped down to the point of oversimplification; in fact, they aren't stripped down at all. They are drawn in as much detail as possible from situations where Game Theory was actually applied by individuals in crisis.

Game Theory was developed and applied to economic problems by two European émigrés, the Hungarian-born mathematician John von Neumann and the Austrian-born economist Oskar Morgenstern. The theory asserts that the same type of analysis that could determine the best moves in parlor games such as poker, bridge, or chess could also be used to find the best strategy in all social conflicts—including international power-politics showdowns such as the Cuban missile crisis, corporate takeover battles such as the Bendix/Martin Marietta saga, and—in the case of this book—personal power plays among employees scrambling for position.

Game Theory has been applied to a large number of major business, political, and military problems: the Panama Canal negotiations, the Camp David agreements, environmental pollution problems, negotiations with terrorists, military problems of search and evasion, advertising battles between rival corporations.

The basic purpose of all these applications is the same—they help those with power to get more of it. This book takes a totally different view. My purpose is to take this weapon of the strong and put it, loaded and lethal, in the hands of the not so strong. My hope is that those who have up to now been on the run from the rampaging powerful, privileged, ruthless, and unscrupulous can turn and fire this weapon, defending themselves and perhaps even bagging the careers of some corporate bullies.

This, I hasten to add, is *not* the point of view of the few existing books that apply Game Theory to business, a couple of which are listed in the bibliography. All of them are written from the standpoint of top management. Why this should be

so I have absolutely no idea since so few are in top management and so many are below them. And judging from widely
respected accounts of declining productivity in the *Harvard
Business Review* and elsewhere, the few at the top have, by
and large, not only made your life miserable, they've also
been doing a pretty rotten job at their own work. To turn
Winston Churchill's remark on its head, never have so many
owed so little to so few.

The Basic Decision-making Principle of Game Theory

Game Theory can be expressed with the horrendous complexity
of linear equations, matrices, and probability vectors. It can also
be expressed with a staggering simplicity that allows its immediate application to practical problems. All of the many applications in this book are based either immediately or ultimately on
one simple, basic principle that will be called The Basic Decision-making Principle of Game Theory:

> **For each of your choices, consider only what you
> don't want but are afraid you might get, and pick the
> alternative that looks best when viewed in this light.**

This principle goes beyond mere worst-case analysis. It also
includes your own intuitive assessment, based entirely on your
own subjective feelings, of how likely it is that you will get what
you don't want.

This book is for those who work *within* a corporate structure. Nearly all of the examples are from the private sector, almost invariably from persons who work at huge corporations in
the United States and Canada. A few examples are from government and the not-for-profit sector. None are from the university,
the military, or the police. Unless I specifically say that I'm a participant, none of the examples are based on my own experience.
They are drawn from the actual experiences of other people
who are not experts on Game Theory, but who have applied the

techniques to their own dilemmas. I think you will recognize many of the situations.

Game Theory lays out in precise, step-by-step detail the mechanisms you need to handle the office politics dilemmas you face. It will *make* you logical, even if you are normally driven by passion, and it does this in a most effective way—it allows you to use logic to satisfy *your* emotional needs. If a decision or an agreement is not true to your innermost needs, what good is it?

The theory raises and answers all the key questions, including some obvious ones that are nonetheless frequently overlooked, such as, "Besides me, who else is making a decision that affects the outcome?" The theory explains how to enumerate and evaluate your options, taking the other guy into account. It shows you how to make up your mind when you are torn between alternatives, and when bargaining, how much to concede and when to dig in your heels. It tells you what information you should give away and what you should conceal, what to believe and when to be suspicious. It also teaches you how to organize the information you already have and where to look for the information you lack.

A good lawyer, or even a bad one, can charge you $125 an hour or more to do much of the same thing, but perhaps not as well. Even worse, you're dependent on him—his schedule, his time, his brains, and his limitations. You merely bring to the issue your money and your problem. At the end of the experience, if you still have confidence in the lawyer, you probably will have too much confidence. You will believe, incorrectly, that your success was based on his insight. In fact, it was probably based on yours. The odds are that he did little more than elicit your feelings about your dilemma so that you could make a decision you could sleep with. But you ended up having more confidence in him and less in yourself!

One goal of this book is to give you more confidence in yourself and less in the experts. You'll still need the experts—the lawyers and the accountants—but you'll be able to deal with them on more equal terms. One should always be wary of benevolent dictators, experts who want to make up your mind and run your life. Often they're like many agents in publishing and show biz—too busy to talk to you when you need to talk to them and guilty of an often heard complaint: "He thinks he's God." But the complaint isn't fair. God has time for everyone.

Part 1
Deciding

2

Figuring Out What You Want and Don't Want

AN EXECUTIVE AT COLUMBIA Pictures once told me that she could guess what her colleagues wanted on any given issue by asking herself only one question: Does this person want to be loved or respected? I protested that the question was of little help in the movie business because virtually everyone in it wanted to be loved. But she insisted that it helped her to eliminate superficial appearances by getting immediately to the hidden agenda. It was, however, of no use in figuring out what she wanted, because although we are constantly enjoined to "know thyself," not many of us do.

In addition to love or respect, people want different things at different times and places in their lives: money, power, adventure, security, parental approval, children, grandchildren—the list is endless. The problem is that to get one thing, one often has to trade off something else, or perhaps even run the risk of losing something of great value. If you have a clear and true sense of what you want, fine; your life is that much easier. But what if you don't know exactly what you want? This is the issue that this chapter addresses, and for which Game Theory can be particularly useful.

Even if you don't know exactly what you want from a given situation, you may nonetheless have one very powerful bit of information—a very clear sense of what you *don't* want. People are often more in touch with their feelings over things they hate then over those they love. For example, have you ever heard anyone say, "I don't know anything about art, but I know what I like"? Invariably they make this statement when standing in front of a painting they can't stand.

This leads us to the First Corollary to the Basic Decision-making Principle of Game Theory:

People are usually more in touch with what they don't want than with what they do want.

This corollary will be used in virtually every example of the book.

This chapter will show you how Game Theory can put your gut feeling to immediate use on your behalf. A specific example will clarify the issue.

The Horatio Alger myth is believed in at one time or another by many of us. With hard work, perseverance, and a proper amount of intelligence, you can get ahead—or so the myth says. And it may still be more true than false. But certainly it's not true for everyone all the time, as some may naively believe. In particular, the myth may be believed a little too literally by those having relatively little experience with it. Women who are working their way up the corporate ladder sometimes make this mistake. Their fathers never thought to warn them, and their mothers didn't know the corporate ropes well enough. So what's a poor girl to do? In a metaphorical, but nonetheless very real business sense, she is an orphan. She's on her own and has to figure out for herself when the myth is true and when it's not working for her. This is the problem of the modern-day Harriet Alger.

Our Harriet began as a secretary at a big office machinery manufacturing company eleven years ago and stayed with the company, working her way up through entry-level training programs and taking advantage of the company's tuition reimbursement program to complete an MBA at night at a local university. Her degree is in finance, so she applied for a position as a manager in the finance department. She had been working in that department for eleven years, and knew it backwards and forwards. The company has a policy of promoting from within—at least at

Harriet's level—and she was without question the most qualified person for the job. But she didn't get it.

Harriet was blocked for advancement by her boss, the vice president of finance, for whom she had worked many years. He saw her not as a dynamic new manager in his division but as his secretary. "She's a secretary, with a secretary's mentality," he told protesting coworkers, who had no doubts that Harriet should have been promoted.

Not surprisingly, Harriet was upset and confused. She had worked hard, done what was expected of her, struggled to advance herself by giving up her spare time and much of her social life, but it had not, so far, done her any good. What should she do? Turn to someone she trusted for advice? This can be a good solution if you've got someone you can count on and whose advice is good. The disadvantage is that it makes you dependent on that person to run your life. For Harriet, however, the point was moot. She simply didn't have anybody she could turn to in whom she had sufficient faith. She'd have to figure this one out herself.

Not that she had any shortage of advice. "Tell that bastard to go to hell," one of her friends said. Another advised her to quit the job at once. Still another recommended she look for and line up another job before quitting her present one. Finally, somebody suggested she fight for the promotion: "You've invested eleven years in this company. You can't flush that away now. You've got to stick up for what's rightfully yours. You can't let these guys push you around; it's a matter of principle!"

It's amazing how much advice one gets from people who haven't put anything in the pot. And basically all the advice did was further confuse her. However, she ran into one person who didn't give her any specific advice; he simply tried to help her sort out the problem herself using Game Theory. He pointed out that all of the conflicting advice indicated one thing—she wasn't trapped. She had plenty of choices. This is an instance of the Second Corollary to the Basic Principle:

You always have choices.

Usually, you don't even have to search for them. They are presented by the carload from meddlesome but well-meaning friends. Always listen to their advice but never take it. Listen for suggestions of choices you might not have even considered. Talk to as many people as you can stand about your problem. This is how you expand your range of options.

Harriet immediately rejected two of the suggestions, telling the V.P. off—"unseemly"—and quitting at once—"I need the money." This left her essentially with two choices: fighting for the promotion or putting all of her energy into finding another job while she held on to her present one. Given these two options, she had to figure out her priorities. Her problem was compounded because she didn't have a clear idea of what she wanted in this situation: "What I had wanted was to put in for the promotion and get it. Everything else in this situation looked lousy to me."

This is an ideal context in which to apply Game Theory, because it deals precisely with a situation where one is most closely in touch with one's feelings—Harriet didn't particularly want any of the outcomes. Harriet applied the underlying principle of Game Theory.

For each of her choices she looked at what she didn't want but was afraid she might get.

First she considered looking for another job: "Sure I'm uneasy about it. I've been at this company eleven years, and I'm not really aggressive about pushing myself. Maybe that's why I've been here eleven years. I know it'll be a lot of work and probably a lot of rejections until I score, but I'm sure if I keep at it I will. So I guess what I don't want but am afraid I might get with this choice is a long search. On the other hand, I'm strong-willed, skilled, I have good training both on the job and from my MBA so this choice isn't too bad, all things considered. I mean, it makes me a little uneasy, but not shot through with loathing, anger, and nervousness."

Next she considered her other choice, fighting for the promotion: "What I don't want but am afraid I might get with this choice is that I'll fight for the promotion and still be turned down. The V.P. might argue with me or ignore me. That's the worst because it's humiliating. At my age I don't need that. I need to have my confidence built up, not ripped down. So this is what really bothers me about fighting for the promotion."

When Harriet used the Basic Decision-making Principle of Game Theory, her choice was obvious:

She should opt for the alternative that looks best when viewed from the standpoint of what she doesn't want but is afraid she might get.

Her decision: She looked for another job—and found a good one five months later.

In this example, Harriet resolved her internal problem—making the decision about what she was going to do—by employing Game Theory. She used the Basic Principle and the first two corollaries.

3

What If You Are Driven by a Compulsion?

IF YOU ARE DRIVEN by a compulsion, your only choice is to follow it—you can't prevent yourself from doing so. No matter how many options you list and evaluate, you will still do whatever your compulsion dictates, so the application of a rational decision-making technique, such as Game Theory, wouldn't *seem* to do you any good.

Not quite. Even if you are driven by a compulsion, Game Theory can be useful. An English movie director I know was in precisely this kind of bind. He had been an extremely successful director of British TV comedy before he got his first big money break—a chance to direct a major Hollywood feature film for theatrical release, a comedy starring a famous, very funny European comedian.

The comedian, however, was very difficult to work with. He wasn't a prima donna; he was too vain for that. However, he did notice if anyone else on the set tried to be funny, and he didn't like it. He wouldn't have any of the other actors fired for being funny, because he was basically decent, but he would pout for a few minutes until he got over the apparent rivalry.

But there was one rivalry he couldn't get over—the rivalry with the director. The real problem was that the director was personally funnier than the comedian. The director, the comedian, and everybody else on the set knew this. Worse still, the director knew that he couldn't help himself—he had to compete with the comedian, and in doing so he was poisoning the air.

This was a catastrophe for the director, who needed to keep the comedian from walking out on the picture in a moment of pique. The director's problem was compounded by difficulties with the director of photography, who acted out his own neurotic problems and constantly challenged the director's ability in front of the crew. They sided with the director of photography since he had employed them on previous movies and seemed more likely than the director to employ them again. "What galls me the most about the director of photography," said the director, "is that I picked the bastard. The producers didn't want him; they thought he was too expensive. But I fought for him because he had photographed a number of very successful comedies. Once he got the job, he figured, 'All right you dumb twit, you don't know anything about making movies, but I do, so you'd better listen to me.' "

What good would listing and evaluating options be to our director? "I tried that, but it didn't help. All of my options were crazy power fantasies—hiring a big thug to accompany me whenever I was around those blokes, carrying a gun, etc. I'd wake up from those fantasies and return to the horrible reality of trying to muscle my way through the picture." Our director finished the movie by virtue of having more energy than anyone else on the set; he simply wore down his opponents. But this was hardly using a strategy, merely a strength that he was fortunate enough to have.

He invited me to the set during the last day of shooting, where I witnessed all of the power struggles. Later, we discussed the politics of the picture. What strategy did he use to finish the picture? "I got my assistant to stay next to me like glue," he said. "Every time the comedian or the director of photography would do something which would have the effect of provoking me, my assistant would whisper in my ear: 'Don't be a schmuck, don't take the bait.' It worked, I was able to get through each day, but I had to get drunk each night to get over it."

Could Game Theory have helped our beleaguered director? Yes, but probably not at the later stages of the movie. His problem was not that of selecting his options but of establishing his priorities. He asked himself, what do I want to get out of this movie? It was the wrong question! He should have asked the opposite question: *What is it about this movie that I don't want but am afraid I might get?* The answer would have been obvious—not finishing the picture.

Whatever he wanted to get out of the movie, one thing was sure. If he didn't finish the picture, he wouldn't get it. And by focusing on what he wanted, he very nearly did not finish the film. He wanted to come in under budget, have a box-office smash, get critical acclaim, and establish a whole new style of comedy. His desire for critical acclaim caused him to ask the director of photography to do things he didn't agree with, and brought on a battle to see who was the boss. And the director's desire to establish a whole new style of comedy put him in conflict with the famous comedian, who wanted the movie simply as a vehicle for his own style of comedy. (To handle this kind of problem using Game Theory, see Chapter 30.) With more experience our director might have been able to achieve all of these goals. But by trying to get all of them, he very nearly got none of them. The movie came in over budget, got tepid reviews at best, and did not establish a whole new style of comedy. It *did,* however, pull in the loot at the box office. As a result, our director's career was established, despite himself.

Game Theory can help, even if you suffer from a compulsion. The theory helps you to take a broader view of the entire project and so to keep your eye on the main risk.

Sorting and Selecting Your Options

OFTEN A PROBLEM IS of a particularly annoying kind; it just hangs around to torment you. The more you think about it, the more options you come up with.

What happens if you have a lot of options, but all of them seem inadequate? Keep looking. The advantage of Game Theory is that it helps you to decide when to stop looking, because it tells you when you've found the right option.

An example of this was the problem confronting Adelaide, thirty, unmarried, and facing continuous, mild, but annoying sexual harassment on her job. She was a financial analyst at a large holding company in San Diego. Basically, she liked her job and got along well with the others there, except for one particularly obnoxious guy, Bret. He was also a financial analyst with Adelaide's rank, and reported to the same director, but was assigned to a totally different area. So their jobs didn't compete, and they had very little occasion to exchange information on the

job. Adelaide found Bret particularly offensive, so this was fine
with her. He leered at the women and was constantly telling
crude, unfunny jokes and making sexist remarks. He also liked to
sarcastically needle everyone around him, but if he couldn't be
the center of attention he'd huffishly turn toward his office,
righteously complaining that everyone was making too much
noise and interfering with his work.

Unfortunately, Adelaide couldn't avoid Bret because they
had adjoining offices and shared a secretary with a dozen
other staff members. Adelaide had developed a standard response to Bret's obnoxious behavior: She told him to cut it
out. He usually got sullen and resentful, and she ignored him.
Sometimes, however, when she was working with the secretary, he'd come out of his office and begin his act with someone else. When she asked him to kindly go to his own office
for these shenanigans, he'd call her various epithets. At first,
Adelaide thought these remarks were directed exclusively at
her, but she found out that Bret addressed them to most of the
women at the office.

Adelaide ignored these remarks until one day something
happened that was too big to ignore. She was working with the
secretary in the hallway when Bret came up, became particularly
obnoxious, and finally provoked Adelaide, who told him off and
said to the secretary that they'd finish the work later, "when
things calm down." However, the secretary got quite agitated,
complained to the manager, and left early. She never turned up
again. Now Adelaide's work would be directly slowed down because of this jerk.

What should she do? She knew about Game Theory and
made a long list of options open to her:

- Quit, complaining about Bret to personnel at the exit interview.

- Complain to the director about Bret.

- File a sexual harassment complaint against Bret.

- Tell Bret to go to hell the next chance she got.

- Send a memo to the manager about Bret to get it in the record.

- Try to meet with Bret and the manager to thrash it out and settle things.

- Do nothing.

Adelaide looked at each option in terms of what she didn't want but was afraid she might get, but none of the options seemed worthwhile. The first did nothing for her, the second left her exposed to the charge of being overly sensitive, and the others had either or both of these faults.

She found a new option on the women's page of the newspaper. An article on sexual harassment on the job suggested a quite different course of action: Write the lout a polite letter on company stationery telling him to cut it out, and send the letter registered return receipt. The Game Theory of this option was brilliant: What she didn't want but was afraid she might get with this letter was that he'd ignore it. She could then use one of her other options, such as requesting a meeting with the manager and Bret to clear the air. She would be fully covered, since she could prove that she had tried to settle the issue outside the framework of the company pecking order, but it hadn't worked.

She sent the letter and was never bothered by Bret again.

In this example, Game Theory helped Adelaide to consider a wide range of options and call her shot very carefully. She was able to weigh each option against its undesired consequences and thus keep searching for a decisive choice, which she soon found.

5

When Your Boss Won't Support You

A LOT OF MANAGERS have gotten where they are by being extremely cautious. Every business decision they make is based on only one criterion—whom will this decision offend? The question may be good for them in terms of their careers, but bad for you if you work under them. Why? Your advancement may require that you accomplish something for the business, and your boss may not let you.

The problem is very often that you don't know all the deals he has made in connection with the current business arrangements. Many deals may have nothing to do with the business itself, but with some outside interest.

For example, a major art museum was designing a catalogue for an upcoming show. The person in charge of the catalogue hired an attractive woman "designer" to do the job. However, she had zero qualifications for the job. Sexual corruption? No, the man who had hired her was gay, but he knew that she owned a large, vacant apartment in a fashionable building, and he wanted a good lease on the place. He got it, and she got the catalogue design job, to the consternation of her so-called subordinates, any one of whom knew ten times the amount she did about designing the catalogue. The frustration they experienced as a consequence was phenomenal. The designer couldn't make any decisions because she didn't know anything, so she constantly hid out. "She was very good at long lunches and sharpening pencils," the subordinate who designed the catalogue told me.

Often you don't know the hidden deals that stymie your career, and there may be no way for you to find out. Perhaps you don't care to know, or perhaps they don't exist—your boss may simply be a jerk. George, twenty-eight, married, with one kid, was in this position. He had no idea why his boss kept blocking his career. George was a media planner at a San Francisco advertising agency, and his job involved recommending various media plans to the clients. But before he could make the recommendation, several persons within the agency had to pass on it. The first of them was his immediate supervisor, who was always very difficult to convince on any new idea. "A lot of times I just duck him when I see him, and then let him know what's what after I've done it," said George.

George saw a chance for a major improvement in the media for a large client, a California importer of single malt scotch whisky. The agency had been using fifteen newspaper ads a week in their twelve best markets. George thought this wasn't very smart. The ads reached only about 25 percent of the country, and most newspaper readers aren't scotch buyers. George figured that the importer would get more coverage for their advertising money if the print ads were placed in upscale magazines that were geared to entertainment and food. The ads would then reach 100 percent of the country and more of the scotch-buying public.

When George told the account executive about his idea, he was asked to put together a specific plan. But his immediate supervisor told him to forget it: "Leave this account alone," George was told. George's dilemma was simple: Should he sneak around his boss and present the new media plan, or should he forget it? He used Game Theory to evaluate his options:

"If I present the plan, what is it that I don't want but am afraid I might get? My supervisor could say nothing, then if the plan is accepted by the others, fine; if not, he'll get back at me later for going against his orders, but what the hell. This is the worst that could happen with this option, because if he speaks out against the plan, then he takes responsibility for squelching it, and I'm off the hook. The same goes if he backs me up, which he'll never do in a million years. The worst, with this option, is if he keeps quiet.

"On the other hand, if I simply drop the new media plan, the worst is that I'm stymied in my job and can't do anything creative or dynamic. This is soul destroying. I'm much better off presenting the plan and facing the music."

This is what he did. Notice that Game Theory, in this case, led to the riskier choice. The decision was true to George. Somebody else might have done things differently. This is an important point about Game Theory. It leads to a decision that is valid for you. Thus, two persons could apply the theory and come up with opposite strategies. No one strategy is best for everyone. Game Theory helps you to find the one that works best for you.

This example illustrates the Third Corollary to the Basic Decision-making Principle of Game Theory:

No one determines by his own actions everything he gets. Other persons also have choices that affect the outcome.

What happened? Since the plan was presented without the endorsement of George's supervisor, the others at the approval meeting backed off. They simply shelved the plan "for the time being." However, the client was approached directly by the magazine advertising salesmen, whom George had tipped off. The client then requested that the agency change the media plan. At this point George saw his opportunity. He and a couple of magazine salesmen had lunch with the head of marketing from the importing company, who offered George a very good job in their own advertising department.

Incidentally, these kinds of career switches are common in advertising. They happen a lot in other fields, too. For example, Eli Black, who put together the United Brands conglomerate, had worked for the bank that serviced the original unit of United Brands. The executives were so impressed with Black that they hired him away from the bank. Everybody usually gains in these situations. The banker gets a better job, the client company gains new talent, and the bank has a friend running a major client corporation, which is infinitely better than dealing with an enemy or a stranger.

This chapter has discussed several lessons from Game Theory:

- **The Third Corollary to the Basic Decision-making Principle shows that you shouldn't expect to always get what you want, even with the utmost calculation.**

- **You may not be able to figure out why your boss won't support you. You can try, but you may never guess the hidden agenda.**

- **The application of the Basic Decision-making Principle of Game Theory may reveal that you should take the riskier choice. This could lead to a change of jobs, perhaps even of careers. Game Theory may make clear to you that you want action, not security.**

- **After applying the Basic Decision-making Principle, you may decide that being stymied is bad, but not as bad as running the risk of being unemployed. Different individuals may come to different conclusions using Game Theory.**

6

When Your Boss Tries to Make You an Accomplice

SOMETIMES BOSSES TRY TO intimidate you into doing things that are against company policy. For personal reasons they try to get you to do something they want, which may definitely be to your ultimate disadvantage. The leverage they have is the implied threat to make your life miserable and perhaps even stymie your career. Bertie, twenty-six, a promising middle manager at the very beginning of her business life, used Game Theory to sort out just such a problem.

Bertie was expecting a desperately wanted promotion and raise. She was an assistant vice president of real estate lending in a major California bank. Her signature was required for all loans issued within her division, and that was the basis of her problem. Her boss, a vice president, had presented her with a $1,000,000 loan request for review. The pressure was on. Not only was the borrower a big customer, but he was the V.P.'s brother-in-law.

This would have been okay, except the loan was far too risky and went totally against the department's lending guidelines. Normally, Bertie wouldn't even have given a loan as questionable as this one any consideration at all. She would simply have stamped it ''rejected.'' Because of the way the organization was structured, she couldn't pass the buck to someone else. Nor could she raise the issue of her boss's pressure at a higher level without running great risks. He would have denied it, and then where would she have been? So she was stuck with only two choices—to accept or reject the loan.

She applied Game Theory by examining each of her choices for what she didn't want but was afraid she might get. She explained what worried her if she turned down the loan:

"It would put me in a bad spot with my boss. He'll make my life hell if I ignore his orders, and he definitely won't recommend me for the raise or promotion. I've been a 'fast tracker,' and this might derail me."

Next she considered what worried her if she approved the loan:

"I know that my boss is being prepared for an East Asian assignment and he may be promoted out within five or six months. If he's gone and with the very big chance that this loan will go bad, I'll be blamed for a lousy credit decision. Even if the loan doesn't go bad, the auditors will certainly flag it, give me static for making it, and put this reprimand in writing in my file. On top of all this, my conscience will unquestionably hound me, which will make me miserable and probably will show up in my work. All of these things make this alternative the worse."

Her decision: "I'm turning down the loan." The key to the application of Game Theory is to *make a decision that is true to oneself.* In this example, Bertie estimated the value of the cluster of things that she didn't want but was afraid she might get if she approved the loan as worse for her than the value of those things she feared she might get if she turned down the loan.

Bertie did one more thing before she put this issue behind her. She set down everything in a memo that she put into a sealed envelope and mailed to herself. She thus had a dated memo to use in the future in case the situation called for it.

This chapter has presented two lessons from Game Theory.

- **You don't have to be intimidated by your boss into jumping into improper action.**

- **You can use the Basic Decision-making Principle of Game Theory to evaluate what to do.**

7

Jumping from a Blocked Path to a Possible Dead-end Job

SOMETIMES THE PROBLEM IN your job isn't that your boss is up to some skullduggery, but that he's simply a plain, ordinary dope. You're smarter, both of you know it, but he doesn't want anyone above him to know it. Otherwise you're likely to get his job and he's likely to get the door. What does he do? Frustrates you. He prevents you from shining by keeping you tied down on the worst projects, the most boring details. And if you complain? It gets in your personnel file as he builds a case against you. The problem can be compounded if you are particularly good at your job. Then your boss can make you indispensable, publicly, by telling his boss about you, "He's indispensable to me. No imagination or initiative, but fantastic at detail." What do you do if your career has been stifled in this way? Change jobs, of course. But sometimes you can do so within your own company.

This can bring up new problems, which call for new evaluatons. Game Theory can be used to evaluate this kind of career jump.

Ed worked in the bond department of a Chicago insurance underwriting company. His boss was incompetent and stifling his career. Ed was an expert at many of the lines handled by the bond department and thus could easily have looked for a job at another company. However, he wasn't sure his boss would give him a good recommendation; he was afraid that the boss would cover his own incompetence by bad-mouthing Ed in a confidential letter of reference.

But Ed did have one exit. He could switch to another division. The one he had his eye on was the property/casualty department. The man in charge there was somewhat sympathetic to Ed and had indicated that he would accept Ed if he put in for the transfer. The problem was that neither his new possible boss nor Ed knew if the company planned to continue in the property/casualty business. They hadn't fully committed to this division, and if the decision went against continuing, Ed could be in new trouble, since the division might simply be folded or at least not expanded. He used Game Theory to evaluate his decision. Ed looked at each of his choices in terms of what he didn't want but was afraid he might get:

"If I stick with the bond department in the hope that my boss will eventually be booted out because he's incompetent, what worries me is that the company will commit to the property/casualty department. I'll have missed the boat and be stuck working for an idiot. That's horrible, even worse when you consider that management would then know that I was unwilling to take a chance. They'd know they could really push me around. It's sort of a choice between a career or a job. I'd have a job but no career.

"On the other hand, if I switch, the worst is if the company doesn't commit to my new department. I could be out of a job—I'd be a trainee so I'd be totally expendable. It's a risk, but at least it's a risk with a chance of getting somewhere."

His decision: "I'd rather run the risk of losing a job than have the sure thing of losing a career." He switched.

Luckily, the company expanded the property/casualty division, and Ed is now doing very well for himself. Incidentally, his old boss in the bond department responded very nastily to the switch, which isn't surprising. Ed, in another division of the company, no longer under his thumb, could blow the whistle on him.

In this chapter, Game Theory was used to clarify and weigh the relative dangers of two unpleasant choices, one involving a

blocked path, the other a possible dead-end job. Analysis of this
kind can be useful for revealing one's priorities.

8

Are You an "Important Person" in Your Office?

SO FAR WE'VE LOOKED at dilemmas where your boss would hold
you in check because of an impenetrable hidden agenda, or because you had frustrated some crooked deal he was trying to
pull, or because he was not very gifted. What happens, however,
if he is very smart and realizes how important you are to him?
The situation can be seductively flattering, until you reflect on
its consequences to your own life.

Walter Kerr, the drama critic, once wrote a column about
"important actors." He was writing about the old English system of actor-managers, in which a prominent actor, a "star" by
our modern usage, would run his own traveling acting company. Naturally, he would cast himself in all of the best parts—
Lear, Hamlet, Macbeth. He would also hire and fire all of the supporting actors.

Who were the "important actors" in these companies?
Whoever they were, the actor-manager who ran the acting company was not counted among them. He was beyond important;
he was referred to simply as "Sir." The important actors, by
contrast, were the reliable folk who could be counted on for a
good workmanlike job in the subordinate roles. Kerr quoted another author, Gordon Craig, in his biography of actor-manager
Henry Irving:

. . . Importance was measured by two negatives. An important actor in an important part was someone who would not call attention to himself and would not blow the play. . . . All plays . . . have dangerous spots in them. Even great plays have moments in which a not very able actor may suddenly seem ludicrous, stopping the stars dead in their tracks and maybe making it impossible for them to regain credibility during the long night ahead. Craig defines a "dangerous moment" as a moment in which Irving was on stage "and about to do some difficult trick.". . . Irving played a lot of melodrama . . . abounding in blood curdling trickery. . . . He certainly didn't want a minor player near him who'd assert himself unduly and thereby break the . . . mood. You don't want a competitor in a spot like that. You want a protective mechanism, and a good one.

What applies to the actor-manager's company applies equally to your office. The actor-manager of your office is probably not the chief executive officer, but perhaps the divisional vice president. In any case, you know who the top doggy is in your immediate office. Unless you're careful you could become an important person to him, in other words, a person held permanently in a subordinate role. To quote Walter Kerr:

Is it possible, in this country and nowadays, to advance from being an "important" actor to being a well-paid one? I suppose the one reason Irving's reliables never escaped a kind of imprisonment was the repertory system itself, operating under a star actor-manager. These players were too useful—even too necessary—in the vital Third Murderer parts to be given a crack at any role that was big enough to take care of itself. And, of course, it was a stable living.

The last thing any of us wants to be in business is a third murderer. But we are so used to self-deception, how do we know if we are typed as third murderers, as important persons? Game

Theory offers a simple test. Consider your present assignment. Suppose you screwed it up. What would your boss say? In other words, ask yourself what it is *he* doesn't want but is afraid he might get. If it is that you might quit, and that he might lose you, then you have become an important person. On the other hand, if he would consider firing and replacing you, then you still have a chance. You have not been typed into a permanent subordinate role. You are not an important person. Thank heaven!

9

Is This Job Offer Tempting Enough?

WHAT HAPPENS WHEN YOU are offered a job that you are tempted to take, but you hesitate because you think there might be an even better job coming up? Should you jump at the offer? That depends on the context and on the pressures on you at that moment. Game Theory can be very helpful in sorting out this kind of dilemma, as illustrated in the following situations.

When You Feel Your Boss Is Killing Your Career with Kindness

Some bosses are very kind, too kind. They look out for your interests even beyond what your interests really are. They go all out, using every contact they have to advance your career—in directions you don't want it advanced. What do you do when you think you are being killed by kindness? Game Theory can tell you if you really are.

Sue, married, no children, twenty-five, used Game Theory to sort out a dilemma posed by what she saw as an overly kind boss. Sue was in sales in a large Texas office-equipment manufacturing company. However, the particular line of equipment she handled was being phased out. Rumors were circulating of reductions in the sales force, at first by attrition and perhaps ultimately by layoffs. There was no chance for a promotion within this division as things stood, and Sue's boss could not even promise that her job was secure in the near term. Sue was on good terms with her boss, who had phoned around to his pals in other divisions of the company in an effort to line something up for her. And he had found a possible promotion to a better sales position in another division. Her potential new boss had interviewed her four times, and her present boss had been told that she would be offered the new job within a few weeks. This brings up her problem.

Sue wanted to switch from sales into the corporate marketing department. She was tired of pounding the pavement and calling on customers. She had gone on a couple of marketing interviews on her own in various divisions within the company. One she didn't get. The other one was a possibility, but not likely. Other marketing jobs might come up, but perhaps not before the new sales job did. What should she do?

Sue used Game Theory to evaluate her options. If a marketing job turned up before she got the formal offer on the sales job, great. Otherwise, Sue had only two real choices: turn down the impending sales job offer or accept it. She evaluated each of her choices for what she didn't want but was afraid she might get:

"If I turn down the sales job offer and nothing comes up for me in marketing, I'm really stuck. My present job will definitely fold in the near future, and my boss would feel I set him up and slapped him in the face by rejecting the job he arranged for me. So I'd lose his support—the only real backing I've got here—and be without a job. I'd be in deep trouble.

"On the other hand, if I accept the sales job and an opening comes up in marketing, am I stuck? Not really. Theoretically, I'm supposed to be committed to the new job for at least six months, but I can always smooth things over. After all, if I switch jobs, I might be viewed as a little bit ruthless, but if I don't switch, I'd be viewed as a dope. Either way is embarrassing, but not catastrophic. It's funny, until I [applied the Basic Principle of Game Theory and] really looked at the risks, I feared this outcome the most—dwelled on it. Now that I bring it out into the open, I realize that it isn't so bad. I guess my boss really is looking out for my best interests."

Sue's decision was to take the sales job. She's still looking for a marketing position.

When You Are Out of Work

One more example of this same kind of problem is useful. We have looked at an example of someone with a job that was rapidly evaporating. How about the person who doesn't have a job but has two prospects? One is immediate, but he's not too keen on it, the other isn't for sure but he'd really like to have it. This was the situation confronting Martin, who had been laid off for about four months because of a corporate merger. He hunted diligently for a job, followed up leads, and went on interviews, but got nothing. He was amazed that he was treated as a pariah even though he had lost his job through no fault of his own.

Finally, he got two offers simultaneously. The first was in Chicago with a major fast-food franchising company and offered everything he wanted—market analysis with some sales, an excellent salary, and good promotion prospects. The catch was that it was offered only conditionally—"assuming everything goes as expected"—and wouldn't start for six weeks. The second job was in sales with a restaurant supply company. The salary wasn't as good as with the franchising job, the work wasn't as interesting, and the financial condition of the company wasn't so hot either. There was a chance the company could fold in a matter of six or eight months. Even more serious, Martin would have to relocate to New Jersey, although the company would pay the expenses. Obviously, he preferred the franchising job, if he could get it.

Martin used Game Theory's Basic Decision-making Principle, examining each of his choices for what he didn't want but was afraid he might get:

"If I take the restaurant supply company's job, what I don't want but am afraid I might get is the knowledge that the franchising job came through. I couldn't really take it. You just can't switch jobs six weeks into a new job—at least I can't, with my record. I'd be stuck, at least for a while, at the restaurant supply company.

"But if I turn down the restaurant supply job in the hope of getting the franchising job, what I don't want but am afraid I might get is no franchising job. It might not come through. A month and a half more of unemployment. I'd be even more in debt than I am now, and I'd have to start all over again looking for a new job. That's lousy, the worst."

He took the restaurant supply company job. Just to hedge his bet, he arranged with a friend to pick up his mail and receive his phone calls, on the chance he might still be offered the franchising job. He figured he could decide then whether or not to dump the restaurant supply company job. But he never got the offer; it went to the son of one of the other managers.

10
Asking for a Promotion

ONE OF THE TOUGHEST decisions on a job is making up your mind to ask for a promotion. Every element of doubt in your personality can work against you. Questions to which you can rationally give a positive answer often elicit an emotional negative one: Can I handle a tougher job? Am I worth more money and responsibility? I know I bluffed my way into my present job and had to

learn on it; can I succeed at this again? The last question is especially pernicious. Few are really qualified for their jobs when
they start them. They've had no experience at them. The rare
person who has had experience usually got it by backing up the
boss—in other words, doing his job. For this honor they usually
get a taste of executive responsibility—the boss blames them for
the screw-ups. They paid the bill but the boss got the lunch. After a while this takes its toll, and people begin to feel they de-
serve only the bill and not the meal.

The hierarchical nature of the organization combines with
your own self-doubts to create in your mind an internalized conspiracy to keep you in line. Your boss almost inevitably feels the
need to assert his authority, which means reminding you constantly that you are a subordinate and that he is your boss. Often
he undermines your confidence, inflating his ego by crushing
yours.

Your problem is to keep your focus on where you want to
be, not on where your boss wants you to be. Game Theory can
be tremendously helpful in clarifying your feelings on this matter, and in so doing the theory can give you amazing confidence. Obviously, a good source of confidence is having many
others seek out your services. But they aren't essential. Inner re-
sources can be even more effective since they are not dependent
on the fickleness of the crowd.

This chapter examines the issue of deciding whether or not
to ask for a promotion. The actual mechanics of how to go about
asking, of how to bargain for a promotion, will be dealt with in
the section on bargaining. At the moment we'll look at the decision itself, examining two alternative situations—one with and
one without an outside job offer in your pocket.

With an Outside Job Offer

Bill was an accounts executive at an advertising agency, assigned
to a steady retailing account. It was a reasonably large account,
but there was very little he could do, as the client was very set in
his ways and happy with the present advertising. This was fine

for the agency but not for Bill; there was no way he could shine. So, two weeks ago, he summoned up his courage and went to his boss to ask for a change to a more dynamic account. This amounted to asking for a promotion, since a more dynamic account could be built up into something bigger, bringing more money into the agency and thereby making Bill more valuable. The account Bill wanted was also in retailing.

His boss told him he'd have to think about it and that Bill should get back to him in a couple of weeks. On the day Bill was to bring up the matter again, he was contacted by another agency, offering him a job with a more dynamic account and for slightly more money. Bill would have preferred to stay with his present agency, providing they sweetened the terms of his job. His question was, should he tell his boss about the outside offer or not?

The decision wasn't obvious to Bill, since he wasn't sure that revealing his trump card would increase his bargaining leverage. He used Game Theory to sort out the decision:

"If I tell him about the outside offer, what I don't want but am afraid I might get is that he'll tell me to take it. He might get his back up over an implied threat to leave. He might not feel like making the effort to go to bat for me, since at this agency they make a big deal about loyalty. That would be bad because I'd like to stay here.

"My other choice is to not tell him about the outside job offer. What I don't want but am afraid I might get with this option is no promotion. He might figure that there is no pressure for giving it to me, or even that I'm not particularly valuable since nobody else is offering me anything. This is obviously worse."

He told his boss about the outside offer. Why did he even hesitate to do so?

"Until I analyzed and focused on what I didn't want, I kept thinking about what I wanted, and that always was getting the promotion without any threats. Things seem to be much clearer if you look at what you don't want than if you look at what you do want."

What happened to Bill? His boss said he would see if he

could get him transferred to the new account Bill had requested. Two days later, he came back to him and said "no dice." Bill is now working at the other agency. The advantage of Game Theory is that Bill was able to go to the new job with the full confidence that he had played out his old job for all it was worth. He had no lingering regrets.

This example illustrates an interesting point about anxiety-producing decisions. When you're on the wrong side of them —in other words, before you've made them—they look terribly complex. But once you've made and acted on them, you wonder what all the fuss was about.

Without an Outside Job Offer

Ken worked in the international division of one of the largest banks in New York. He hadn't been promoted in over two years, but felt the time was right. Why? "I just completed a huge loan package, and I should use it to bolster my case for a promotion. The problem is I don't know how this will be viewed by senior management. Maybe they won't respond gracefully to pressure from a subordinate."

Ken spent a long time arguing that the only way he could "win" this game would be to sit back and have the promotion handed to him. "Otherwise, if I pressure them and they give me the promotion, I'll never know if they really consider me a valued employee or are just trying to avoid a pain in the ass."

As soon as Ken applied Game Theory and looked at what he didn't want but was afraid he might get, his decision became obvious:

"If I ask and they turn me down, that's lousy, but at least I know where I stand.

"If I sit around waiting, I may never get the promotion and may never really know how I stand. This is obviously the worse situation. What the hell am I sitting around here thinking about it for? It's obvious that I should ask."

But it became obvious only when he used Game Theory's Basic Decision-making Principle, stopped dreaming about what he wanted, and focused on what he didn't want but was afraid he might get. When we compare these two examples, and the lessons from Game Theory that they contain, we find that the issue of an outside job offer is not the key to asking for a promotion. The two critical issues are:

1. Do you feel you are entitled to the promotion?

2. Do you want to know how you stand?

If the answer to both questions is yes, ask for the promotion. If not, don't ask.

11

When Your Authority Is Challenged

EVERY NEW EXECUTIVE FACES the problem of establishing his authority. Ben was the new controller at a rapidly expanding cable television company. Because of the fast-paced growth, the physical plant of the company kept growing. New buildings were rented or bought and then modified and redecorated (no time to build from scratch). All this capital expenditure was beginning to eat into profit. This brought the purchases to the attention of the parent company, which insisted on a new policy: All purchases of fixed assets had to be approved by the cable company's controller.

Ben had been at his new post for two days when one of his clerks who dealt with accounts payable flagged an item: The V.P. for administration, in charge of purchases, had ordered

a new carpet for his friend, the V.P. for marketing. Both of them
were old-timers at the company, which didn't exactly mean they
were *old*. The V.P. for administration was only twenty-eight,
and the V.P. for marketing was a gorgeous woman of thirty-two
who, unlike the many other women at the company, may have
gotten to her present position by sleeping her way into the job.
Anyway, this was the office gossip, which was reinforced by her
appearance. She usually wore half-unbuttoned blouses and was
known around the office as "The Dish." Ben didn't want to get
on the bad side of either of them, especially "The Dish," because he was not sure who was protecting her at the company.

What should he do? Ben used the Basic Decision-making
Principle of Game Theory to sort through his problem.

"Sure I can pretend this happened before I got the job, but if
I don't do anything, what I don't want but am afraid I might get
is that these two V.P.s won't take me seriously. I can't let them
simply ignore the rules I'm supposed to enforce. Eventually this
sort of thing will get back to corporate, where I'll be viewed as a
weak guy. And they want somebody to tighten the grip on this
company. So not taking action is bad, really the worst thing for
me.

"But if I come down on them for this, what I don't want but
am afraid I might get is that I'll be viewed as a boring accountant,
a spoilsport. There really is a 'corporate culture' here. Everybody tries to pretend they're ultra-hip. Besides, what the hell
can I do? It's ridiculous to have the carpet returned, and for all I
know she needed it. I never saw her office before. Also, I don't
want them going to the president on this. I'd win but look as if I
couldn't handle a simple little thing." Game Theory clarified
that he had to do something and that whatever he did would
have to be handled with a light touch.

He finally paid personal calls on both "The Dish" and the
V.P. of administration, and had them sign requests for retro-
active approval. Word got out that he was a decent guy who
would approve reasonable office improvements but would also
personally, but not publicly, embarrass people who didn't fol-

low corporate procedures. He was never challenged on this issue again.

12

Speaking Up or Keeping Silent

YOU WANT TO ADVANCE your career as quickly as you can. Your
strategy is to try to offend no one, if you can live with yourself at
the same time, and wait for the right opening. In the meantime,
you'll try to do as good a job as you possibly can at your present
assignment. However, you not only must do a good job but must
also appear to do a good job. This may not be so easy. Others in
the company will be only too happy to pin the blame for their
mistakes on you.

This is precisely the situation in which Ann found herself.
She tried very hard not to make any waves, but suddenly found
herself in a situation where it looked as if she would have to.
Game Theory was critically important to her.

Ann was the special projects manager for the Houston office
of a very large air freight shipping company. In fact, she had
helped set up the office two years before. Now Ann was put in
charge of setting up a new telephone system for this office. She
researched the options and recommended a certain kind of
equipment. She felt that the acceptance of her recommendations
was very important, because she was afraid she would be held
accountable for the success of whatever equipment was chosen.
Ann was certain that merely being covered with written memos
would not be adequate. The system simply had to perform effectively. However, corporate rejected her recommendation in

favor of another system. She figured she had to go along with their recommendation and make the system successful.

She did, for two months, until the building was literally washed away in a flood that accompanied a major hurricane. They moved into temporary quarters and had a new telephone system in operation within a few days, this time with the brand of equipment she had wanted—it was the only one available on such short notice. So now she had her whole set-up exactly as she wanted it, and it worked fantastically. Productivity increased, costs decreased—an efficiency expert's dream come true.

Six months later the old offices had been restored and everyone was gearing up to move back in. Ann had to present a study of the results of her telephone system. She was happy to do so, as the results vindicated her recommendations. She urged that the permanent office be equipped exactly like the very successful temporary one. The regional executive assured Ann that they were fully behind her approach. "Corporate won't push us around," she was told.

The next week, the vendor of the telephone equipment phoned her. He was threatening to repossess all of his equipment because corporate had neither paid for it nor even signed the contract. Ann found out later that corporate had never read any of her reports. They had always planned to stick by their original choice.

Ann was appalled, and she demanded that regional stand up to corporate, as they had promised to do. Needless to say, they didn't. Ann's boss spoke to Mr. Johnson, the deputy regional vice president—useless. Johnson lived up to his reputation of being an ogre.

In the meantime, Ann had lost credibility with her own staff. They were demoralized, for it seemed to them that no matter how good a job they did, their work would not be appreciated. It was very difficult for Ann to motivate them, to maintain her ability to function with her unit, and to be able to talk to other suppliers of office equipment. Ann used Game Theory to work out whether or not she should approach Johnson.

She decided she had three options:

- Keep her mouth shut.
- Take it up with Johnson.
- Go over his head to the regional vice president.

"If I go over Johnson's head to the regional vice president, what I don't want but am afraid I might get is total disaster on my job. Johnson will be furious and put pressure on my boss. Eventually I'll be ruined. So this option is totally out.

"If I do nothing, what I don't want but am afraid I might get is not only a complete lack of self-respect, but also the respect of my unit. And without that, I'm through here. The work will suffer. And even if nobody here gives me any credit if the work is good, they'll sure as hell give me plenty of blame if the work is bad. So this option is virtually as bad as the first one.

"If I speak up, taking up the matter with Mr. Johnson, what I don't want but am afraid I might get is Mr. Johnson's wrath. But who knows? Maybe I won't outrage him. And this is my only chance at keeping my credibility with my unit. It looks as if I'll have to speak to the old bastard. And I'll have to do it publicly or else my unit won't believe I did it."

The interesting thing about this application of the Basic Decision-making Principle is that it leads to the outwardly riskier choice. Game Theory is a cautious approach to problems, but sometimes it recommends risky choices, depending on your values and the pressures upon you in the situation.

Ann got her chance to speak publicly to Johnson the following week, at a major regional meeting. He gave a high-sounding speech about increasing productivity, working together, improving the quality of life, and openness and honesty in working relations.

She approached him after his talk to invite him to visit her temporary office. He told her to forget any changes but agreed to visit her office to review the telephone system. Essentially he told her he didn't want to buck corporate over such a small matter.

Later, she found out from her boss that Johnson had spoken

favorably to him about her. Johnson admired her for speaking up. She lucked out on this, since the fellow was unpredictable. Incidentally, her own staff also gave her the respect she needed to do her job properly. So the whole situation resolved itself and she was back to her original strategy of waiting for her break to make her move.

There are several lessons from Game Theory in this chapter:

- **Maintaining your credibility with subordinates may force you to speak up to an office ogre.**

- **The application of Game Theory's Basic Decision-making Principle may indicate that the seemingly riskier choice is, all things considered, the more cautious one.**

- **The ogre may be unpredictable, and thus the ultimate result of your choice may take a while to develop.**

13

When You Have to Force an End to a Problem

MIDDLE MANAGERS ARE USUALLY under tremendous time pressure. Reports have to be written, decisions made, deals concluded. To succeed at their jobs they need good staff support, but they don't always get it. For example, a hard-pressed middle manager can lose his secretary for any number of reasons, but two stand out: The secretary is too bad or too good. Too bad is understandable, you fire her. But too good? That can be a problem because your boss may steal her. It's not couched that way: "We have to do what's best for the employee, so she can grow with the firm," your boss piously tells you. But what about *your* growth within the firm?

That's your problem. To solve it you have to replace your secretary. But now you are hampered by corporate procedures. You can't simply call an employment agency and start interviewing. That would be too rational, too businesslike. No, your company is organized along the principles of the Argentine civil service—whatever could be done in an hour must take at least a month. In the meantime, your productivity sinks, along with your career.

The problems often begin with the personnel department. They must first post the vacancy internally for three days to give present employees a crack at it. This sounds fair enough, except that it may take them two days (or more) to get around to posting it. Now you have gone a week without a secretary. Even worse is the frustration of dealing with personnel. They never inform you of what is going on, usually because nothing is.

Another week can go by. Yes, you are permitted to hire a temp during this period; but the temp must be trained. Temps garble telephone messages. And temps have been known to be rude to the wrong people. So many middle managers forgo the privilege of hiring a temp. Instead they hound personnel.

This was Rita's situation. She was part of a seven-manager, three-secretary department. That's what it was supposed to be. Three weeks before, her excellent secretary had been promoted, becoming her boss's secretary. In addition to the boss's secretary-napping, another full-time secretary had quit without notice. So seven managers were down to one secretary, who seemed to favor the work of one particularly handsome male manager. There was a suspicion of hanky-panky but no proof. In any case, six managers, including Rita, were hurting for secretarial assistance.

Rita pestered personnel to fill the two vacant slots. Nothing. Finally, a secretary in another division heard about the problem.

Her friend, Babs, was looking for work. Rita interviewed her. Babs was good, although a bit talkative, maybe even too talkative, and she had no business experience. So she'd require special training. On the other hand, she met the other requirements: She was willing to work, to learn the office word processor system, and she seemed to get along well with the managers and the other secretary.

Rita now had to make up her mind. Should she continue hounding personnel or settle for Babs? Game Theory's Basic Decision-making Principle helped her sort it out:

"If I reject Babs, what I don't want but am afraid I might get is either no candidates from personnel or ones that are lousier than Babs. Either way, I'm without secretarial assistance. This is suicidal for my career.

"If I hire Babs, what I don't want but am afraid I might get is that Babs won't work out. Then I can be sure of no further 'help' from personnel, not that they've been worth a damn so far. In fact, all they've done is keep me from having a secretary for the past two weeks. So the worst that can happen if I hire Babs is that I'm in the same spot I'm in now."

Game Theory's Basic Decision-making Principle made her decision clear: Hire Babs and to hell with personnel. Incidentally, this decision worked out all too well. Babs did talk a bit too much, but also was terribly efficient and hardworking, so much so that Rita's boss mentioned her to a friend, who promoted her out of Rita's department.

The lesson in this is contained in a line from a Bessie Smith song in which she cautions women that if they want to keep their men, "Never tell your friends what your man can do." The wisdom applies with only slight modification to middle managers with good secretaries: Never tell your boss what your secretary can do.

14

When You Have to Fill a Vacancy Right Away

A GOOD FRIEND RUNS one of the largest independent pharmacies in Boston. He has forty employees, and if he finds somebody good he's always hiring. Always hiring? What if there are no vacancies? He hires anyway. "There's always a turnover, so I rarely have to fire the incompetent ones." It sounds cruel but it isn't, because he pays extremely well, higher than anyone else does for comparable work in the area. Essentially, he's always auctioning off his jobs to the highest bidder in terms of energy, enthusiasm, intelligence, and so forth.

He can get away with it because he owns his own business. If you don't, you can't, although occasionally executives try and then let personnel sort it out. But even without a display of brazen callousness, you can do some of the things our Boston pharmacist-entrepreneur does. You can always interview. Had Rita in the previous chapter done so, she wouldn't have had to rely on an incompetent personnel department. Interviewing takes time, but not as much lost time as being stuck in the crunch without proper assistance.

Consider a simple application of Game Theory's Basic Principle: What is it you don't want but are afraid you might get if you interview when you have no vacancies? In addition to losing a little time, perhaps a very good job candidate will get fed up with you. And if you don't interview? You probably will never even meet that candidate, but you may very well end up without adequate supporting staff. Which is worse for you, the routine loss of a little time or a major loss of staff just when you need it?

Despite the obvious logic of interviewing all the time, a lot of executives don't do it and end up in new dilemmas.

For example, Joyce ran the St. Louis branch office for a nationwide ballroom dancing school. She was two days away from going on a much-needed three-week vacation when one of her instructors gave notice: "Don't take it personally," he told her, "I'm moving to California." She didn't take it personally, since she couldn't stand the guy and was glad to see him go. But she had to replace him before she left or the company would lose the income he generated. The school's selling point was one-on-one instruction. Joyce had not been routinely interviewing, so she suddenly had to try to find someone.

Through one of the other instructors she got a prospect who was qualified and eager to get started. Joyce offered the same salary as that of the instructor who had just given notice. No deal. Joyce would either have to pay more and thus reduce her profit margin, or reject this person and probably get no one in time, thus reducing her total potential revenue.

Looking at each of her options in terms of what she didn't want but was afraid she might get revealed two poor alternatives:

"If I hire him, what I don't want but am afraid I might get is that the other instructors might also ask for more money. That's bad.

"If I don't hire him, the company probably loses out on business. From the point of view of reporting to headquarters, that's worse."

Why?

"When I return from my vacation, the shoe will be on the other foot. I can explain to the new instructor that he either gets paid the same as the others or I'll have to replace him—which I'll be able to do, because I'll be here in town."

Game Theory reveals a very unpleasant situation, which did not have to exist in the first place. Joyce could have changed the situation by anticipating what it was likely to be. To accomplish this she need only have worked out the simple piece of Game

Theory described at the beginning of this chapter, and routinely interviewed whether or not she had an opening.

15

Drinking with the Boys

GETTING ALONG WITH YOUR boss and coworkers often involves more than merely doing a good job at the office. You often have to demonstrate that you like to be with them, and the only way you can convince them of that is to spend time with them outside working hours. This is sometimes referred to as "making Brownie points." The implication is that you are doing something that you would rather not be doing in order to butter up people you would rather not be with.

If this is completely true, you're in the wrong business. But often it's only partly true. You like the people, but you don't like the kind of socializing they do.

For example, your boss and colleagues go for drinks after work and invite you along. If you consistently decline, they may think that you don't want to be around them. Their suspicions may not be true, but if this goes on long enough, you may as well kiss the job at your company goodbye.

Sarah, thirty-two, married, had this predicament. She had a very good job as the stylist for a famous line of sheets produced by one of the largest textile manufacturers in the world. She had a staff of ten designers working under her and was constantly in meetings with corporate bigwigs. This led to her problem: These guys liked to drink, and after work they went to a fancy bar across from their office building and downed a few rounds. They liked Sarah and always invited her along. She'd stagger home from these sessions too dazed from alcohol to enjoy the rest of the evening. After a few of these episodes she begged off. But this began to produce friction. The boys began to treat Sarah as though she were no longer one of the boys.

She applied Game Theory to her problem:

"If I go for the drinks, what I don't want but certainly will get is wrecked for the evening. This isn't doing my health or marriage any good.

"If I don't go for the drinks, those guys are going to treat me as an outsider, which is no good for my career."

Both of her options were equally bad.

She needed a new strategy, one which demonstrated that she wanted to be around the boys but which didn't wreck her marriage or give her a perpetual hangover. She needed something that would open a bank account of good will with her colleagues, in which she could store up good will, and then draw down on the reserves when she turned down their drinking sessions. As she thought about her dilemma, she realized that she was treating it as a passive problem—she would accept, and much more often reject, someone else's invitation. She liked the boys, but she didn't like their after-work drinking. Why couldn't she invite them to something she liked? This way she could also include her husband in the socializing. Sarah analyzed this strategy using Game Theory:

"If I invite them to events of my choosing, what I don't want but am afraid I might get is that they won't like my choices. But at least they'll know that I wanted to be with them, which is the whole point. And I won't feel dragged along to something I don't want to go to. So it reverses the situation for me. Also, if I pick the events carefully, they might like them. In any case, this is obviously better than either of my other choices."

The one problem with Sarah's strategy is that it can be expensive. She had to research it carefully to make sure that it wasn't beyond her means. She was able to find excellent concerts at very reasonable prices. Although this was New York

City, with its nearly unlimited variety of entertainment, other places also offer quality events at low prices. For example, most universities throughout North America have concerts by visiting maestros, and all of them have sports events. One enjoyable, memorable evening can make up for a hell of a lot of skipped, after-work drinking sessions. Naturally, the evening has to be enjoyable and interesting, so it has to be tailored, to a certain degree, to the tastes and interests of the boss or colleagues.

Sarah's strategy didn't really involve making Brownie points. She was now doing what she wanted to do, so the unpleasantness normally associated with the term doesn't apply. Incidentally, her new strategy turned out to be extremely successful, and she and her husband now go out fairly often to plays, concerts, and movies with her colleagues and her boss. And she almost never drinks with the boys anymore.

There are several lessons from Game Theory in this chapter:

- **You could find yourself in an unpleasant dilemma between socializing with your boss at events you can't stand, or turning down his invitation and getting him fed up with you.**

- **You always have a third strategy of inviting the boss and colleagues to social events of your choosing.**

- **A couple of memorable events can set up a bank account of good will that you can draw on.**

16

Not Taking the Fall

AFTER THE BAY OF Pigs fiasco, President Kennedy said on television that although everyone wanted to be identified with success, "failure is an orphan." Did he resign? No, he went on with the rest of his speech. At a critical moment during Watergate, President Nixon said on national television that in any organization the man at the top ultimately takes full responsibility, "and I take full responsibility." Did he resign? No, he went on with the rest of his speech, and stayed in office for a few more months.

The man at the top may bear full responsibility, but that rarely keeps him from staying at the top. President Truman once put a sign on his desk: "The buck stops here." Truman apparently lived up to both the letter and spirit of his desk sign. But many other top executives polish such signs to such a degree of brightness that they blind the viewer to what is really going on.

So much for the big shots, what about those who are still on the way up? Should they emulate the great and stoically take full responsibility for their mistakes? A lot of office sharpies are aware that this sometimes works. After all, to err is human but to forgive divine. Honesty may not only be the best policy but also the most effectively manipulative. Bosses sometimes like to forgive those who show themselves to be weak and helpless. It puts the boss in a paternalistic role, which many bosses find very comfortable. The trick seems to be to confess *before* the boss discovers your mistake. Otherwise you've been caught out, and there is a hint that you wouldn't be contrite if you didn't have to be.

The Game Theory of this is rather interesting. Your choices

are to admit to your mistakes or to try to pretend you didn't
make them. If you admit to them, what is it you don't want but
are afraid you might get? A reprimand? Likely. Fired? Unlikely
but possible, depending on the severity of the error. So the absolute worst is that you'll be fired. If you try to stonewall, on the
other hand, what is it that you don't want but are afraid you
might get? Fired, because you not only were incompetent but
also dishonest. You decide which is worse.

But with half the sharks in the company running around
confessing to their all too frequent mistakes, what about the guy
who has to decide whether or not to deny someone else's mistake? Suppose one of your coworkers made an error that gums
up your work. *He* made the mistake, but superficial appearances
indicate that you did.

This is the situation Jack found himself in. He was the company's budget manager and was in charge of preparing the
budget for the next fiscal year. After he prepared the budget for
an upcoming corporate meeting, he discovered that some of the
figures supplied to him were incorrect, so his final budget figures were wrong as well. Rather than dumping the problem back
in the lap of the man who supplied him with the bum data, Jack
immediately went ahead and started correcting the budget. That
was at six o'clock on a Friday night. Everyone but Jack had gone
home. Jack's boss had snuck away so Jack couldn't tell him what
had happened; even a written memo wouldn't be seen until the
boss returned. In the meantime, the worldwide review meeting
would have to be delayed for a week—an embarrassment, to say
the least. Jack's pickle was even more severe: The man who gave
him the poor information was away on vacation for two weeks,
and thus not there to answer the charges.

Jack used Game Theory to analyze his situation:

"If this guy were here and admitted his mistake, which I'm
pretty sure he would do, everybody would be off the hook. Nobody gets fired at this company for admitting their mistakes. But
the bastard is out backpacking someplace! So either I tell on him
or keep my mouth shut and take the blame.

"If I tell, what I don't want but am afraid I might get is that he'll say he told me he wasn't sure of his data, but didn't have time to check it over before going on vacation. The higher-ups might then think I am partly to blame and am just trying to pass the buck. They hate that at this company, so I'd eat it and I don't want to. I'd also probably have to keep working with that idiot after I fingered him, which wouldn't be a lot of fun.

"But if I don't tell, I'll get the blame for total incompetence—delaying a worldwide meeting—and I'll really be screwed. That would be the worst, since I'm responsible for preparing the budget."

Game Theory's Basic Decision-making Principle made clear to Jack that he couldn't allow himself to be pinned with the blame, especially since he wasn't responsible. But he still wasn't happy with the alternative strategy—nailing the other guy. So Jack thought for a while and came up with a third strategy. He took the blame and passed the buck simultaneously. How did he do this? He blamed the error on the other guy, but admitted negligence in not checking the data before writing up the budget. Checking the data was not part of his job, and his bosses all knew it. So Jack got to:

1. confess and put the bosses in a position where they could forgive him for not doing something that was above and beyond the call of duty, and

2. pass the real blame on to where it was deserved.

Game Theory showed the need for a new strategy, and Jack got off the hook.

When a Friend Asks You to Cover Up His Error

Occasionally a person you work with asks you to go out on the limb for him. Often the person is on your level, has made some kind of error, and asks you to be an accomplice in covering it up. Sometimes, the myth of colleague solidarity is invoked: "We're both in the same boat." He usually leaves out that it's a leaky lifeboat about to be cast adrift. At other times a vague deal is suggested: "One hand washes the other."

But what do you do if the request comes from a genuine friend who is in real trouble? You can save your friend's job but at the risk of your own. This was the situation in which Joan found herself. A year ago, Vera had helped her get her job at a large Boston bank. They did the same kind of work for different supervisors. They were close friends but didn't really work together. Vera had had a rough year: a divorce, illness. Perhaps as a consequence, she had been a bit negligent in processing the papers for an employee of a corporate client. Vera had put this person's whole file under a stack of papers and forgotten about it until it was too late for him to qualify for a tax credit.

The only way Vera could be sure to cover up this error was to ask Joan to prepare a complex calculation and send it directly to her, without notifying either supervisor. This action would be totally flouting company procedure, but probably wouldn't be detected. Nor was it likely that the victim would realize he had been deprived of a tax benefit, since his taxes were quite complicated and probably not subsequently checked by another accountant.

Joan discussed her options in terms of what she didn't want but was afraid she might get:

"If I provide the calculation, as requested, I put myself in a terribly exposed position. I'd have participated in a deliberate attempt to deceive. If that were ever discovered, I could be finished not only at this job but at this career. I might even be sued by the client for the loss of the tax benefit.

"If I don't provide the calculation, Vera runs the risk of getting caught, but at a mistake, not a fraud. I could lose a friend, but if I explain to her what the comparative risks are, I think she'll understand that she's asking me to carry a greater risk than she herself would under these circumstances. Besides, she might not even get caught on this. I hope not."

Game Theory helped Joan weigh the competing claims of friendship and professional risks and ethics. Joan didn't provide the calculation. Vera was angry, but eventually got over it, especially since she never got caught on the incident.

There are several lessons from Game Theory in this chapter:

- **The application of the Basic Decision-making Principle of Game Theory shows that denial and cover-up is generally not a rational strategy. This is true not because "honesty is the best policy" or any such moral homily, but because the downside risks are greater with dishonesty, and because most bosses want to have the godlike power to forgive.**

- **Sometimes you have to point the finger, but you must do so in a way that does not look like buck-passing.**

- **Use the Basic Decision-making Principle of Game Theory to evaluate carefully any requests from colleagues to help them out in their cover-up. Your analysis will probably reveal that it's not worth it, and that they are asking you to carry a greater risk than they do themselves.**

Part 2
Dueling

17

From Deciding to Dueling

SOMETIMES MAKING UP YOUR mind is only half the battle. Literally half. The other half belongs to the other guy—your rival for promotion, power, money, position, or whatever. He has choices, too. And if you are both scrambling for the same slice of the corporate pie, you're in a duel.

Can you still use the Basic Decision-making Principle of Game Theory? Sure, but so can he. Who's going to win? That depends on how well each of you plays the office politics game, and on the underlying strategic nature of the situation. If you both use Game Theory effectively, the only way to tell in advance who will win is to see who is favored by the game itself. Some situations will be rigged in favor of you, others in favor of the other guy, and some will be stalemates.

Take poker, for example. Just because you're a strong player at poker doesn't mean you always win. The cards you're dealt also have something to do with the outcome. A strong player at poker usually picks his games carefully. If the cards aren't with him, and he's up against other strong players, he gets out of the game. Office politics works exactly the same way. A strong player at the game of office politics picks his battles very carefully, with the aim of avoiding those that show poor prospects. Game Theory will allow you to size up the situation and try to avoid showdowns where you seem likely to lose.

What happens if in your office politics showdowns you use Game Theory and your rival does not? You'll probably beat the pants off him. But maybe not. The situation may be so heavily rigged in his favor that even a complete fool could beat you.

What happens if he uses Game Theory and you don't? It's just as before, except in this case, the odds are, you'll lose.

The Free Trip to Acapulco

A huge mutual insurance company has a division devoted to agency operations, and executives spend a lot of time scheming up incentives to increase business. They've come up with some doozies: awards for size of sales, bonuses for specific, very high production targets, and, most successful of all, dismissals for failure to meet the production goals.

All of the various schemes have one thing in common—a ranking of who's doing what and for how much. After all, insurance companies are always ranking customers according to risk, so why not turn the same actuarial guns on their own staff and rank them according to success?

The list is posted. Everybody knows how everybody stands. What could be more open, more aboveboard, and, in particular, less susceptible to the intrigues of office politics? So far, so good, but now comes the zinger—the week-long, all expenses paid trip for the winner and his or her spouse, first class to Acapulco. The trip goes to the top twelve district managers. The company has hundreds of districts around the country, but only the most successful twelve managers go on the trip. They get even more. If they make the top twelve, they become eligible for the next opening as an agency manager. We're now talking about the lower end of top management—the big time.

Somehow, Hal, thirty-two and a district manager, made it— barely. He's Number Twelve. Now the duel begins. It will be waged between the last person eligible for the trip to Acapulco, Hal, and the one who just missed it, Number Thirteen. The time is early December, and there is still a chance to change the name on the twelfth slot. Only one of these two can occupy that spot, and both of them want it.

At first nothing worse than a factory speed-up occurs. Company underwriters are pressured or begged to issue policies by the last day of the month. New salesmen are sometimes added to the district at the last minute under one pretext or another. Sales territories are juggled. But both Hal and Thirteen can do this, and both of them will, so things stay the same, until the game escalates. Each has one additional strategy, to place extra risky business—the law firm down the street where all of the eighty partners have pacemakers.

The risks are high—expense to the company, lawsuits, even dismissal—but so are the stakes. Winning this contest is very nearly the only way to get a shot at top management. The choices for each of our managers are to take only the usual moderate risk (it is impossible to take no risk in this business) or to take an ultra-high risk. The game is simple to score as shown by the following scorecard:

- If both Twelve and Thirteen take moderate risks, Twelve keeps his place and Thirteen loses.

- If both Twelve and Thirteen take ultra-high risks, Twelve still keeps his place and Thirteen still loses, because Twelve was already there and has matched Thirteen's risky strategy. (What might happen to both of them six months later, when their chickens come home to roost, is a future problem.)

- If Twelve goes for ultra-high risk, while Thirteen sticks to the usual moderate risk, Twelve wins again.

- Only if Twelve is moderate, but Thirteen goes for broke with ultra-high risks, can Twelve be knocked off the list and replaced by Thirteen.

That's the game.

We are now using our Third Corollary to the Basic Decision-making Principle:

No one determines by his own actions everything he gets. Other persons also have choices that affect the outcome.

Your job is to figure out who they are and what they can do. For Hal, Number Twelve, the competitor he has to watch out for isn't Number Eleven, he's already in the gravy. It's Number Thirteen. *He's* the threat. Is there a test using Game Theory to figure this out? Sure, apply the Basic Decision-making Principle to each of these potential rivals. With Number Eleven, what is it that Hal doesn't want but is afraid he might get? Nothing—there is absolutely nothing Number Eleven can do to him. How about Number Thirteen? *He* could knock Hal out of the twelfth spot.

Next, Hal has to figure out his strategies. We've done that in lots of examples so far, and in this case it is particularly easy—he can take an ultra-high or a moderate risk. And so can Number Thirteen. Then all Hal has to do is make a simple list, of the kind we have just done, to look at the combinations of different strategies. Most of the time, you won't even have to write it down, but it usually helps.

What should Hal do?

"If I take a moderate risk, what I don't want but am afraid I might get is that Number Thirteen will take an ultra-high risk and I'll lose. That's a disaster. I mean, I'm winning today, how can I let this bum beat me in three weeks?

"On the other hand, if I take the ultra-high risk, what I don't want but am afraid I might get is that Number Thirteen will take only a moderate risk. I win the trip to Acapulco and a shot at top management, but at the ultimate risk to my whole career. That's not so good."

Which is worse?

"I can't let that cheapskate beat me. I'm going to win this contest. I'll take the ultra-high risk."

So far, this looks like any other decision-making problem. But it's not quite over. The man in the hot seat has an active opponent. How do you know if you have an active opponent? That seems like a silly question, but as we shall see in several later examples it isn't silly at all. In the meantime, the answer to the question is: Use the Basic Decision-making Principle of Game Theory. But you've just used it? Use it again, this time applied to the decision you have just made:

If you use the Basic Decision-making Principle of Game Theory, what is it that you don't want but are afraid you might get? For Hal the answer is all too clear: His rival will figure out what he is planning to do, and then he will use Game Theory after Hal does in order to beat him at his own game. If Hal weren't careful, this might be possible under certain circumstances. Let's see if the Trip to Acapulco Game is one of them:

Number Thirteen knows the score here just as well as you do.

"Sure."

He can figure out your best strategy, just as easily as you can.

"Right."

So as long as you are being super-competitive and taking ultra risks, he's going to lose the contest anyway. If he wants to avoid what he doesn't want but is afraid he might get in the long run, why shouldn't he protect himself by taking only moderate risks?

"He should if he's got half a brain."

Then why should you, if you figure him to switch to moderate risks, run ultra-high risks with your own career?

"You're right, I should cover my own ass and switch to moderate risks, too."

Of course, he can then switch to ultra-high risks and zap you.

"But then I can switch back to ultra-high."

And then he can switch back to moderate risks.

"What the hell do I do?"

Here is Corollary Four to the Basic Decision-making Principle:

You may be perfectly rational to be torn between alternatives even after you have carefully evaluated them.

Game theory can tell you when you are in one of these spirals. The theory will tell you when you can stop racking your brain to find a best strategy because there is no best strategy.

The key to winning the Trip to Acapulco Contest for Hal is to try to find out what Number Thirteen is up to. In short, Hal should cheat. But how? There really isn't any way to get the information early enough to do anything with it. Lunch with the underwriters isn't good enough. They might not remember, they might confuse Number Thirteen with some other guy. There is no practical way to cheat, to find out.

Hal could ask Number Thirteen, but it wouldn't work. Let's pretend they're both in the same city and Hal knows Number Thirteen well enough to ask him. What's he going to ask him: "Are you taking dangerous and unnecessary risks with the company's assets?"

"Who, me?"

Let's say he got over that problem somehow. Would Number Thirteen tell him the truth? Would you, if you were Number Thirteen?

Let's say Number Thirteen tells the truth. Would you believe him if you were Number Twelve? Are you kidding?

There doesn't seem to be any way to cheat in the Trip to Acapulco Game. If there is no way to cheat, is there a way to keep Number Thirteen from cheating? Yes, here's what Hal has to do: He must keep what he is doing secret from Number Thirteen.

That's the basic idea. How this can be implemented will be discussed in later chapters, but for the moment the advice is: Keep your mouth shut.

Okay, we now know how to keep Number Thirteen from cheating Hal, but how can Hal be sure of winning? The answer is, he can't. The odds are very good that Hal will win this game, but it's not for sure. Number Thirteen might still sneak in and steal the twelfth spot if Hal decides to be cautious. This game is like poker or baseball; there is an element of uncertainty as to exactly what the other guy is up to.

Which choice did Hal finally make, the moderate or the ultra-high risk? He gave it all he had and took every risk he could find. So he held on to Number Twelve. He found out later that this was a good choice—four other guys were tied for the Number Thirteen spot. Each of them went for broke, which is what some of them are since their business soured. Hal lucked out—none of his business turned out to be so bad that he was fired.

There are several lessons from Game Theory in this chapter:

• **Some large companies, through sales incentives programs, literally set up duels such as that confronting rival baseball team managers at the bottom of the ninth.**

• **If you are a contender, you can use the Third Corollary to the Basic Decision-making Principle as a guide to figure out who your rivals are. For each of the other contenders, ask yourself what you don't want but are afraid you might get. This will help you to zero in on the one you have to worry about.**

• **Even after rationally analyzing all of your options, you may still be torn between alternatives. This is okay. Your reason hasn't failed you. Rationality itself can't provide a clear answer. Don't feel inadequate. You would be inadequate if you thought you could think your way out of the dilemma.**

• **If necessary, make up a scorecard composed of your choices against those of the guy you have to worry about.**

• **One thing you can do is to keep your mouth shut about your intentions.**

18

When to Lie

THE LAST CHAPTER SHOWED how a huge mutual insurance company had set up a game exceedingly close to a tied, tense baseball game at the bottom of the ninth. It wasn't this way for everyone, just the two men who got caught up in it. Keeping their mouths shut turned out to be clearly to their advantage. This isn't always the case. Sometimes you can get caught in a duel where not only can you not keep your mouth shut, but the written rules forbid it.

Don, thirty, had been in personnel in a medium-sized home furnishings textile company. When the company folded, he had to get another job fast, and he did, working for the government of a major western city. It wasn't a final resting place for his career, but it wasn't a bad place to wait out hard times either.

Now Don is the assistant personnel director for a department of this city. Don specializes in hiring "provisional" employees. Those are people hired in the absence of a roster of civil service "eligibles," to use the jargon thrown around Don's office. In other words, no person currently on the civil service lists fits the bill, so Don's job is to find somebody who isn't currently on the list. He puts ads in newspapers, gets on the phone to college placement offices—all the usual things he used to do in private enterprise. Things aren't done that differently in government.

They are, however, on those occasions when Don has to hire from a list of civil service eligibles. Now the written rules enter.

The rule that causes the most complication in Don's job is the "rule of one out of three," as the people at the office call it. A government agency has to make up a list of eligible candidates and actually hire one of the top three candidates on the list. This seems like a perfectly reasonable law. It gets around the "brother-in-law" problem and allows the government agency some flexibility in case the man at the top of the list, or even the next highest, is a total incompetent. It also causes a lot of problems for an honest guy like Don, who wants to do a good job while he bides his time and looks for the kind of job he really wants in the private sector.

The rule of one out of three actually breaks down to the following subset:

- Don has to make an offer to the first, second, or third candidate, in the order in which they appear on the list. In other words, he can't skip down to number four or below.

- After he offers a job to number one, the other two head the list, and number four becomes number three.

- A candidate is always free to turn down a job offer, but he gets penalized for doing so. The penalty is that he's dropped from the list—a pretty rough price for freedom of choice, but that's what it is. This is good for Don because he can move on to the next candidate. This helps him to make room among the top three, in case all of them are turkeys.

- Suppose Don thinks the top three candidates are horrible. He does not have the option of dropping them from the list, but he does have one other trick up his sleeve: judged, but not chosen. This is a civil service euphemism meaning "skip this jerk for the good of the city." The guy doesn't get bumped from the list, and Don can move on to the next one of the two remaining top candidates. The catch is that Don may use only two consecutive "judged, but not chosens" in a row, and thus cannot use this ploy to work his way past the top three to get to

number four. This could well guarantee that at least one
person judged by the interviewer to be incompetent will
be hired by the city that day. If Don uses up his "judged,
but not chosen" quota, he either has to hire a jerk or stop
interviewing.

Assuming the top three candidates on the list of eligibles
should really be ineligible, Don's problem amounts to this: He
should try to get as many of the bad candidates as possible to reject the job, and he should at the same time use as few "judged,
but not chosens" as possible.

To clarify these rules, let's say Don thinks candidates one,
two, and three are stinkers, but candidate four is great. His goal
is to offer the job to number four. The question is, how? Don can
judge, but not choose number one, and do the same with number two. But this leaves him stuck with the third turkey. He has
to hire him or not fill the job. The latter is a totally unacceptable
option from Don's point of view since it looks as if he's not
doing his job; there is no way he can cover himself on paper if he
doesn't hire somebody. Of course, the third turkey might turn
down the job, but he might not, too.

This is a bad spot for Don. The only way he can try to get
out of it is by offering the job to the third turkey, but in a way
that makes it look very unappealing. Don uses the well-known
technique of the negative interview. We all know what this is.
Don stresses the total absence of prestige, the rotten work envi-
ronment, and the absolute lack of hope for promotion that this
job allegedly involves: "It's only fair to warn you that this is the
kind of job where a guy like you can expect to be 'pissed on and
passed over,' as we say here at the agency." If this isn't enough,
Don emphasizes the technical job information that the candidate
lacks, and points out very forcefully that the job involves a pro-
bation period, after which unsuccessful job holders will be summarily fired, and this information will go into their permanent
records.

When confronted with a lousy candidate, Don's real options come down to this:

- Don can judge, but not choose.

- Don can offer the job and make it seem as repulsive as possible.

That's it. He has no other real options.

"If I judge, but don't choose, what I don't want but am afraid I might get is that the guy would have turned down the job anyway. This has happened to me in the past. I give the turkey the negative interview, but don't think it's working. I'm afraid he doesn't believe me and will accept the job if I offer it. So I tell him we've looked him over but aren't picking him. I give him the form for this. Then he tells me he would have turned down the job anyway because he was afraid he'd have been fired from it, but he was stringing me along to stay on the eligibles list. And I've blown half of my quota of passes. This is extremely lousy.

"On the other hand, if I offer the job to the turkey, what I don't want but am afraid I might get is his acceptance. Then I've brought another dud into the agency. This is actually the worst, since for me the rock bottom is to hire deadwood. It looks bad for me and goes into my own evaluation file. So anything that stalls that is better."

Don's best strategy is to choose judged, but not chosen.

But if the "eligible" figures you're going to do that, he should make sure you do by making it look like there's no question he'll take the job if it's offered.

"Right, but if he does that too much I figure he's bluffing, and I offer him the job."

But then he should accept the job.

"He might, but if I figure he'll really accept it, I should do a judged, but not chosen."

Do you mean that if the turkey indicates he really wants the job, you assume that he really doesn't want it?

"Yes, and vice versa. If he sounds as if he really doesn't

want it, I assume he really does. That's why these job interviews with rotten candidates go on for so long. If the guy's good the interview is over in ten minutes. If he's lousy it can go on for two hours while we dance around, trying to figure each other out.''

The civil service rules have set up a totally unstable situation that forces both a conscientious personnel manager and a desperate job applicant to attempt to deceive each other.

What should Don do? As with our last example, the Trip to Acapulco Contest, no single strategy is best. And, as with that example, Don must keep his intentions secret from the job applicant. He must cultivate his best poker-face manner.

This game is very similar to a battle of baseball managers where one switches pitchers to outmaneuver a heavy hitter, but the other then puts in a pinch hitter to throw off the pitcher. This can go on until one side or the other runs out of players. There is no natural ending point. In the civil-service hiring game both Don and the turkey can try to give false signals to the other, and each in turn can respond to the other's false signals. But knowing this gives Don the real advantage. He can keep the game going as long as he likes. He can interview the candidate all day. His aim is to get the candidate to announce: ''I don't want the job.''

These are the lessons from Game Theory for this kind of situation:

- **Recognize that you are in a situation that has no best strategy.**

- **Realize that lying is not only acceptable, it is absolutely essential to success in this kind of situation, where you literally didn't make the rules but your career could die by them.**

- **Recognize that you control one key variable—the ability to end the game whenever you choose.**

19

When to Be a Bastard— Dueling over Personnel

IN SOME VERY LARGE organizations bureaucratic rules get so entrenched they lead to inefficiencies, but surely these organizations are the exceptions. Private enterprise simply can't afford to permit silly, personally vicious games to occur. They're bad for the bottom line! The board of directors and the principal shareholders would be up in arms, at least if they knew about them. And, eventually, somebody always blows the whistle.

Oh, yeah? Let's look at another personnel example, this one from private industry.

Gus is a manager in the personnel department at an oil megacorporation. His specialty is hiring a certain kind of geologist. And his career is in jeopardy because of a vaguely similar, but much more vicious, problem than that described in the last chapter.

Gus is contacted by somebody in the oil exploration department. The caller has found somebody for a job that he badly needs. Inevitably, Gus knows that this is a pal of the caller's and a favor is being done. Would Gus please interview this guy right away and hire him? "Sure," Gus has to reply, "send him over. If he meets our guidelines and qualifications, he's yours."

There's just one hitch. Exploration is also supposed to send over a written requisition requesting the hiring of this candidate. And, technically, Gus doesn't have to interview him until he gets the requisition. Gus tried to enforce this formal requirement when he first got on the job. His supervisor, the guy who was promoted out of the job Gus now occupies, set him straight:

"We've got a billion-dollar exploration project going, and you want to hold it up for a lousy requisition form? If you want your papers in order, get a job working for the city. Here we get the job done. You interview that geologist right now. The damn paperwork can wait."

Now the game begins. Gus interviews the geologist. It doesn't matter to Gus if the guy has three heads, Gus should hire him if the exploration department sends over a requisition. Otherwise Gus can be accused of obstructing the guys in the field. There is no greater crime at this company. But Gus must make the decision to hire before he gets the requisition. Doesn't he always get the requisition later? Unfortunately, no. Sometimes, in fact, often, it never comes at all. There are various reasons for this:

- A sudden budget cut forces exploration to cut back unexpectedly.

- The exploration budget wasn't adequate for this candidate to begin with, but nobody checked before sending the guy over; this happens all the time.

- The candidate was sent over as part of a power struggle within the exploration department. The faction that sent him over lost.

- Somebody in the exploration department simply changed his mind and wants personnel to cover for him.

- A grudge match. Somebody in exploration wants to embarrass Gus. This happens but not often.

Gus describes his problem:

"If I hire the guy, and exploration doesn't send over a requisition, what I don't want but am afraid I might get isn't all that bad, providing it doesn't happen too often. The hired geologist can always be transferred for the time being. If worse comes to worst, I can take him out for a drink and tell him the job has been eliminated, but we'll definitely keep him in mind for future jobs. And usually I do, so this isn't too bad.

"But if I don't hire the guy, what I don't want but am afraid I might get is that exploration does send over the requisition. That's big trouble: obstructing the guys in the field."

There shouldn't be any problem. The Basic Decision-making Principle of Game Theory shows that Gus should always hire and sort out the problems later. For a single shot of the game it is a very good strategy. But in the long run it can cause problems:

"I did that for a year, and it got me into a lot of trouble. I was hiring too many geologists."

Gus applied the Basic Decision-making Principle of Game Theory a second time. He asked himself, if I use my best strategy and always hire, what is it that I don't want but am afraid I might get? The answer became clear the moment he asked this question:

"What I don't want but am afraid I might get is that if I always hire any joker they send to me, they never have to send over a requisition unless they damn well feel like it, which is almost always after I've hired the guy. If they know I've hired him, it's to their advantage to wait to see if they really need or want him. That way they don't risk anything. They can send over candidates at the drop of a hat and know that I'll hire them without their taking any chances. Because I'm completely predictable to the guys in exploration, they're always in the clear and I'm always putting my butt on the line. Of course, if I know that they're not going to send over a requisition, then I shouldn't hire the candidate. So it's kind of circular. But realizing that showed me the only way I could force them to think twice about their requests for hires was to turn some of them down. And that's just what I did, I started turning down a few of the geologists who came in without requisition orders. And when the exploration department didn't get a couple of the guys they wanted, they screamed, but they also started to behave. It took me a while to realize it, but the way things are around here, it actually pays to be a bastard some of the time."

Do you mean you turned down candidates and then subsequently got the requisition? Isn't that the worst thing?

"Yes, I just had to tough it out, and I did. The key was that they couldn't be sure I would approve everybody they sent over, so they started being more careful. If you think about it, this game is weighted very heavily on my side. I look good in each situation unless I turn down somebody for whom they later send over a requisition. That's the only time they can catch me out. The irony is that although they win the power struggle at that moment, they lose the overall game by calling attention to the fact that they have been trading on my good nature and have been pulling a power play. It makes them look like jackasses for a while. So they start behaving and sending over requisitions, and I start being a nice guy again and hiring everybody, so they stop sending the requisitions and the whole thing starts all over again."

In this kind of situation, Game Theory provides a number of lessons:

- **The corporate culture of your company, the unwritten law, may force you into a bind where none of your choices seems any good, if the other persons at your company know what you are going to do.**

- **The strategy recommended by the Basic Decision-making Principle of Game Theory is always a good strategy for the short run. But in the long run, it may require re-examination.**

- **If this is the case, simply apply the Basic Decision-making Principle of Game Theory a second time: If you use your best strategy, what is it that you don't want but are afraid you might get?**

- **If the answer to the second application of the Basic Decision-making Principle of Game Theory is that everybody can predict what you are going to do,**

**then stop being predictable. Use one of your other
options occasionally.**

- **If being unpredictable means occasionally appearing to be a bastard, go ahead and be a bastard.
  You may have occasionally to act in a ruthless
  manner not because this is your nature but because
  the rules, written and unwritten, at your company
  give you no other choice. If you want to hang on to
  your job, you may have to be a little bit ruthless.**

20

When to Lie to Your Boss, Case 1—Your Boss Is Badgering You for Information

RULES, WRITTEN AND UNWRITTEN, can put you into a not so funny
bind. We've seen examples in a big insurance company, a big
city government, and a big engineering company—all big organizations. Is bigness the problem? Anonymity, alienation, the machine steamrolling over the lone individual? Let's make sure.
Let's look at a little example, but within the corporate structure.
We'll make it an all too common situation:

Your boss hates your guts. He wants to fire you, but he can't
without a good reason, or at least a good pretext, and to get that
he needs evidence. He could get that by compiling a dossier with
letters of complaints from outsiders. This is a common enough

practice in academia, where bosses (deans, department chairper-
sons, etc.) often feel they have nothing better to do with their
time than to encourage poison pen letters. But in the private sector bosses are supposed to be too busy for such pettiness. They
have to come up with some other source of biased information,
such as you. They have to try to hang you with your own work.

This is Paula's situation. Her boss, Dee, hates her. Why? Dee
is ruthlessly ambitious and believes Paula is lining up with Dee's
own boss, Greg, a general manager, to block her advancement.

Dee, extremely pretty, has been accused of using her sex appeal to get ahead in the company. Paula, on the other hand, is
not so pretty, in fact a bit on the plain side, and although ambitious, is not ruthless about it. The firm, a personal-care products
company, rarely promotes women beyond first-line supervisory
positions. However, there are rumors that this might change,
and a number of women supervisors, Dee among them, might
get promoted. Greg sees Dee as a potential threat to his own position. He's not out to get her; he simply ignores her as much as
he can. He does this by going around her to Paula and encourag-
ing Paula to go around Dee directly to him. What can poor Paula
do? If she tells Greg that she has to work through Dee, he'll think
she's a fool, and her chances for promotion would be nil. This is
especially true since Dee, as we noted, can't stand Paula, and in
fact wants to get her fired. Dee has not exactly been a model
boss. She has taken full credit for work done by Paula, bad-
mouthed Paula to anyone who will listen, and once even gave
Paula incorrect information, so Paula could report the bum data
at a meeting and look like an idiot while Dee sat there, smiling.

Greg called in Paula and assigned her the Smith project,
which should have gone to Dee. Paula had just finished a cost
study, and now Greg wanted her to complete that work by writing up a report advocating a specific choice of suppliers and
spelling out her reasons for the choice. The project involved a
massive amount of money. Why didn't Greg assign the report to
Dee? In addition to the rivalry reasons, he knew he could bully
Paula into changing the report if he didn't like what she wrote.

Dee could go over his head, and he wasn't about to let that happen.

The day after Paula got the assignment, Dee left a memo for her: "Update me on Smith project." Dee was going to browbeat her into telling which supplier she was going to recommend. Then Dee would either attack that choice in her own oral report or support it, claiming that she had really set Paula straight on it. This way Dee could claim credit.

Paula, by then, had in fact made her selection, let's call it the Chi Chi Corporation. They were more expensive than the alternatives, Old Source, Inc., and Silicone, Inc., a new supplier. But Chi Chi offered other advantages: guaranteed delivery dates, very good service, and a reputation for performance.

Paula's question was: Should she tell Dee that she had opted for Chi Chi, or should she lie?

Paula analyzed each of these choices using Game Theory's Basic Decision-making Principle:

"If I tell the truth, what I don't want but am afraid I might get is that Dee will *defend* my choice at the later staff meeting, claiming credit for suggesting it. There's no question she will. She's done it before. It's not exactly good for advancing my career.

"If I deliberately lie, what I don't want but am afraid I might get is that Dee will attack my choice, badger me into owning up to my real choice, or even worse, tell everyone at the staff meeting that she suggested it and that I originally wanted to go for one of the other companies. She'd claim credit again, and I'd get to listen to her lecture me."

Which are you going to choose?

"I don't know, they're both lousy."

If Paula had moral scruples against lying, she'd have had no problem. She'd simply have told the truth and let Dee rip off the credit.

Paula realized she needed a new strategy, one that she hadn't previously considered as a way to break out of the circularity of her problem. How did she come up with a new strategy? She applied the Basic Decision-making Principle of Game Theory a second time: If she used either of her strategies—they both were worth the same to her—what was it that she didn't want but was afraid she might get? In the one case she got ripped off, in the other caught out. So she realized she needed a strategy with which neither undesirable outcome happened:

"I won't get caught out if I don't tell a lie, and I won't get ripped off if I don't tell the truth. This can happen if I don't say anything."

As with the case of the construction company's personnel department, secrecy, being unpredictable, was a real asset. The problem for Paula was that her original two strategies didn't allow her to be secret. Game Theory showed that she had to find a way to do this. The theory didn't tell her how; she had to come up with the gimmick herself. But the theory pointed in the direction she had to look.

She applied the Basic Decision-making Principle of Game Theory to her new option of keeping her mouth shut by whatever means:

"If I keep my mouth shut, what I don't want but am afraid I might get is that Dee will accuse me of being uncooperative. But everybody knows we don't cooperate anyway. So I just have to do this in a way that Dee can't really even accuse me of it."

Paula sent Dee a memo saying she wasn't feeling well and would have to go home, but hoped to see her before the staff meeting the next day. Of course, Paula didn't see her before the meeting. She showed up just as it was about to begin and gave her report. Dee could say nothing.

In this kind of situation, there are several lessons from Game Theory:

- **A power struggle can put you into a bind where none of your choices seems any good.**

- **The Basic Decision-making Principle of Game Theory may not be any real help the first time around, since it may recommend more than one option.**

• **You can use a second application of the Basic Decision-making Principle to point you in the direction in which you will find a new strategy.**

21

When to Lie to Your Boss, Case 2—When Your Boss Controls the Agenda

SEVERAL CHAPTERS HAVE SHOWN that secrecy is not necessarily a symptom of paranoid behavior, as your detractors may claim, but is instead a rational response to an irrational situation. The last chapter showed how to handle the situation in which the boss tries to wheedle information out of you. His aim is to make you look bad in the eyes of his own boss.

Your boss can also use secrecy as a weapon against you. The crude way is to withhold information from you. However, this strategy leaves him open to the charge of deliberately obstructing your work. A much more subtle way for him to operate is not to request key information from you until the last possible moment, when it is too late for you to gather it. Then he can fault you for not having it.

One way he can do this is through his ability to set the agenda. He can tell you what to do and when to do it. But what if he leaves the agenda open? The real power the boss has is in not revealing the schedule to you until it is too late to act on it. This way, he can catch you and make you look bad.

This was the situation confronting Alicia, a manager in

the real estate lending department of a huge Miami bank. She was supposed to manage a staff of seven, but due to attrition, the actual number was down to four. The problem was compounded by the success of her unit, which had almost tripled its business in the past year. Her unit was overworked, to say the least.

Alicia managed the real estate loan business for three countries—Trinidad, Barbados, and Grenada. Part of her responsibility was to prepare lengthy annual business plans for the real estate business in these countries. The Grenadan plan presented no problems. Because of Grenada's political situation, her bank did hardly any business there, so she always got that plan out of the way in no time. But she had been so overwhelmed with routine work that she hadn't had time to prepare the plans for the other two countries and was late with them. Her boss, who had been wanting to get rid of her for a long time, saw his opportunity.

Here's how he planned to do it: The reports were always delivered at a meeting with her boss, and his boss, the V.P. in charge of international real estate loans. The meetings never lasted more than an hour, and under no circumstances was the report for more than one country discussed at any given meeting. This was because the V.P. always wanted at least a few days to digest the information and then come back with questions. Otherwise he felt that it looked as if he didn't know what he was doing, which he didn't, but that's another matter.

Alicia was highly regarded by this vice president, but he couldn't be counted on to understand the pressure and time constraints under which she was forced to operate. This is where Alicia's boss saw his chance. He asked Alicia to prepare next year's strategic plans for both Trinidad and Barbados, and have them ready for a meeting the following Monday. On paper, he had informed her of the agenda, but in reality he had not, since only one of the national reports would be discussed. Furthermore, Alicia couldn't possibly prepare both reports because of the pressure of her day-to-day work. At best she could prepare only one of the plans, which would be fine because only one would be discussed at the meeting with the V.P. But which one?

Alicia asked her boss. "I'll leave it to you," he said with a smile. She knew what that meant. Under the guise of being democratic, her boss was waiting to find out which plan she had prepared, and then he would ask her to report on the other one. He then left town on a business trip. Alicia discreetly phoned a friend, the private secretary to the V.P., to see what was written on his calendar. Useless! No new information. Alicia was totally on her own.

She used Game Theory to sort through her problem:

"If I prepare the plan for Barbados, what I don't want but am afraid I might get is that my boss will ask me to report on Trinidad, which would be very bad. I'm from Trinidad and they sort of expect me to be able to plan in detail at the drop of a hat just because it's my own country. So not having the plan for Trinidad would probably be the worse.

"On the other hand, if I prepare the report for Trinidad, what I don't want but am afraid I might get is that my boss will ask for a report on Barbados. This would be pretty bad, too. He'd say something like, 'Sure, she can report on her own country, but she's not really up to snuff when it comes to other countries.' "

Which is worse?

"Not having the Trinidad plan would make me look worse, but it's not that simple. If my boss figures I have the Trinidad plan, he'll ask for the one on Barbados, and vice versa. Whatever I do, I'm caught."

Is there any way you could prepare less detailed strategic plans on both countries?

"I could prepare them, but it would certainly ruin my career. Remember, they discuss only one country at each meeting. So a sketchy plan on that country would make me look very bad, probably get me fired. I mean it's better to have a good plan for the wrong country than a lousy plan for the right one."

By using the Basic Decision-making Principle of Game Theory, Alicia realized that no strategy was best for her in this situation. The interesting thing here is that the boss didn't want to know which country she was going to report on. Why? She could then confirm the discussion in a written memo; this way she couldn't. Whenever your boss doesn't want information that presumably is in his interest to know, watch out! Alicia's boss would want to know, eventually, just before the meeting. Then he could use the information against her.

Couldn't she take the initiative and send him a memo that nailed down which country she would report on? She could, but it wouldn't do her any good. Her boss could feign ignorance of the memo until after the meeting. If she carbon-copied the V.P., her boss could claim she was trying to circumvent his specific verbal orders. Her boss set the agenda, and there was no way for her to usurp that prerogative and get away with it. So she was stuck with secrecy. Her boss had used it as a weapon against her.

This was the next lesson that Alicia learned from Game Theory. She asked herself the following question: "Once I've written the strategic plan, what is it I don't want but am afraid I might get?" The answer was obvious: Her boss would find out just before the meeting and at that time would ask for the report on the other country. She would lose for sure. Otherwise, she would have a fifty-fifty chance of preparing the report on the right country.

So her strategy was clear. She had to mislead him just before the meeting. Here's how she did it. First, Alicia did her report on Trinidad, the country she knew best, and also the one called for by her use of the Basic Decision-making Principle of Game Theory. Next, she put all copies of her written plan in a large manila envelope, which she sealed up tightly. On the outside of the envelope, she wrote in big bold letters

"Barbados." Alicia arrived a few seconds late to the meeting and put the envelope on her lap where her boss could see it. She made sure he'd look by wearing a short skirt. He read "Barbados" on the outside of the envelope, took the bait, and asked for the strategic plan for Trinidad. She opened the envelope and gave it to him.

Later, the V.P., who wasn't aware any of this intrigue was going on, asked her why the outside of the envelope said Barbados while inside was a report on Trinidad. "Oh, that was just a note to myself to tell you that next time we could talk about Barbados," she replied.

These are the lessons from Game Theory for this kind of situation:

- If your boss could give you a specific agenda but doesn't, watch out. He may be setting you up for the kill—he may not be also, so be sure you know his intentions.

- If at first the Basic Decision-making Principle of Game Theory doesn't lead to a satisfactory decision, realize that this situation requires secrecy on your part.

- Once you are aware of the need for secrecy, reapply the Basic Decision-making Principle of Game Theory to the problem of keeping your choice secret. This should establish that you don't want to tip your hand until it is too late for your boss to do anything about it.

- If you know what your boss is thinking, you might be able to mislead him by giving him false signals. You have to do this without lying.

22

How to Confound the Worthless Sons of the Filthy Rich—When They Work for You

THE FACT THAT SOMEBODY nominally is called your subordinate doesn't make it so. You may not have chosen him. He may not faithfully execute your orders. Somebody else may be protecting him. But you may nonetheless take the rap for what he does. After all, you're supposed to be his boss, and responsible for what he does.

The subordinate isn't loyal and does a lousy job, but you can't fire him; he has drag, a relative in the business. Sometimes the relative isn't even in your company, but is a powerhouse in the whole industry. If you fire the worthless nephew, tongues will wag, and what they spit out may not reflect favorably on you. There's always a chance, of course, that the uncle thinks his nephew is a jerk and should be fired. But how do you know for sure? The safer strategy is to keep the bum on the payroll.

Sound familiar? This is the problem Alex, thirty-two, had. He was an assistant V.P. of marketing at a major motion picture studio. Two months after he got his job, a supervisor's job opened up in his department. Alex's boss, Sam, insisted that Alex interview the applicants. He didn't tell him why until after he hired Jock (not his real name, but an accurate description) over Alex's objections:

"Jock is a jerk!"

84

"Maybe so," replied Sam, "but he's your jerk now. He reports to you."

Jock, the son of a very famous and extremely powerful woman in the industry, gave an entirely new dimension to the term "vulgar slob." He carried a large shopping bag full of health-food-store prepared sandwiches with him wherever he went. And he gobbled them up all day long. He didn't let the requirements of holding a conversation slow him down. He would stop only to run in place or jump rope. In addition, Jock was reckless in everything he did and made an endless series of expensive errors, most of them over and over. When called on his appallingly bad work, he would reply with a muscle-bound shrug.

Unfortunately, his antics made things look bad for Alex, who was, after all, his boss. But Alex had very little recourse. Firing Jock was out of the question. Even routinely reporting Jock's bad behavior had become dicey. Sam, who was only eight years older than Jock, had taken a fatherly shine to the boy. Sam was not an entirely indulgent surrogate father. Although at times tender, he would sometimes cruelly upbraid him.

Jock soon realized that he could largely ignore the complaints of his nominal boss, Alex, and go directly to Daddy Sam. And Sam let him do it. Jock became known around the office as "the Son of Sam."

Alex's problem: He was taking the rap for Jock's errors. Alex used Game Theory to figure out his best strategy for dealing with this problem. He figured he had three options:

- Be laid-back with Jock, and pray for the best.

- Be tough with Jock, with the goal that he would completely change his personality and do a good job.

- Be tough with Jock and then explain why to Sam.

Alex analyzed each of his choices using the Basic Decision-making Principle of Game Theory:

"If I take it as it comes, what I don't want but am afraid I might get is that I'll be a schmuck. Jock isn't going to get better on his own, and I won't even be able to pretend to myself that I'm his boss. So this is no choice at all. I won't even consider it.

"If I'm tough, with the goal that he'll get better, what I don't want but am afraid I might get is that he'll run to Sam and cry about how I mistreat him. Then not only will I not get any improvement out of Jock, but Sam'll give me a lot of heat about the lousy job I'm doing managing Jock, and how I should stop pushing him around. I'll get blamed for Jock's screw-ups and scolded for criticizing him. The worst of both worlds. This would be insufferable.

"If I'm tough with Jock and then immediately run to Sam to lay out my side, what I don't want but am afraid I might get is that Jock won't run to Sam to complain. He doesn't always. I'll be admitting to Sam that I can't manage Jock—everybody knows that, but I'm not supposed to admit it—and I've run to defend my actions when I didn't have to. But this isn't as bad as my second choice."

Then you always use your strategy of slamming Jock and telling Sam why?

"I tried that for a while, but Jock caught on. He started not running to Sam to ask for protection. I looked consistently foolish in Sam's eyes. Sam would say, 'What the hell's wrong with you that you can't manage a little spoiled kid?'

"The situation is circular. If I tell Sam, Jock is best off not complaining. If I don't tell Sam, Jock is best off running to him. As long as Jock knows what I'm going to do, he's got me."

Game Theory offers a solution: utter randomness. Alex must be totally unpredictable. That way Jock can't take advantage of Alex's actions by anticipating them and running to Sam. He can run to Sam any time he wants, but he'll do so at times when Alex hasn't already been there. In this way, Jock will look like a crybaby, and Sam will begin to get disgusted with him. Jock, of course, will never be fired, but he will be neutralized.

Alex figured that simply flipping a coin wouldn't be good enough. He thought he was better off explaining to Sam more often than not, but not all the time. This way he used his best Game Theory strategy, but not exclusively.

This is literally what he did: He took a deck of cards, removed about half the red ones, shuffled the deck, and then asked Jock to pick one. Alex had previously decided that a black card would mean he should explain to Sam about Jock, and a red card would indicate that he should not explain. Jock picked one of the black ones, so Alex went to Sam to explain. The next time Jock acted up, Alex went through the same routine, but this time Jock picked a red card so Alex didn't explain to Sam. Jock never figured out what the cards were about, nor could he predict what Alex would do, so he started to refrain from complaining to Sam so often. Sam got the impression that Alex was now in control of the situation, which he was, by being randomly out of control.

These are the lessons from Game Theory in this type of situation:

- Unlike some previous examples where secrecy was called for, this situation will be endlessly repeated.

- Your boss will be keeping score, but he will likely be judging the situation using an overall impression. Therefore, your goal should be to win in his overall impression, not on any specific round.

- Since you probably can't get The Worthless Son of the Filthy Rich fired, your goal should be to neutralize him.

- Your only chance at neutralizing him is if you are unpredictable. This will have two benefits. First, he can't anticipate your actions. Second, since he won't be able to figure you out, he'll probably think you're a little bit irrational, a little bit nuts. This will cause him to fear you.

- **Don't be afraid to be a little bit nuts. This is one of the few ways you can get respect.**

23

Hard Times and Layoffs— Somebody Has to Go: Making Sure It's Not You

EVER BEEN THROUGH A retrenchment in your company? Everyone's scared. Rumors flourish. The executions are random, unpredictable—almost.

Actually, they're not all that random. Sometimes they are predictable and therefore perhaps avoidable. In your panic, you might ask yourself a simple question: Could your job be combined with someone else's? Of course it could—everybody's could. The new job might be horrendous for the poor sucker who has it; it might kill him, but at least he'll die with his boots on instead of with his feet dangling idly in the stream. He'll die working.

The real question to ask yourself is: Has my job ever been combined with someone else's? Whoever will propose the truncated reorganization will want to stick out his neck as little as possible. One surefire way to avoid sticking out one's neck is to claim precedent. The courts have been using that for centuries. So can your rival. Rival, what rival? A guy with two kids, an unemployed wife, and a ferocious mortgage, and at the same level in the organization as you. He may propose the return to the old organizational structure.

Finding out if you have a rival is a simple matter. Simply

consult the organization chart. If there is someone on your level, find out who he or she is, fast. Next, ask an old-timer at the company how things were organized in the past. If your rival heads a division that was once part of your division, you may have a problem.

This is precisely what happened to Gloria, head of the local division of the customer service department of a moving company. Her rival, Mr. Mortgage, headed the other division within the customer service department, the long-distance division. Both were headquartered in the same building in a midwestern city. Gloria and Mr. Mortgage had the same immediate boss. Four years earlier, before either Gloria or Mr. Mortgage had joined the company, the two divisions were combined into one, which was simply called the customer service department. The department was broken into two divisions as the long-distance operations got bigger and bigger. Until Gloria asked around, she hadn't known this. But Mr. Mortgage apparently did, because prominent in a report he wrote was the suggestion that the company return to its original organizational structure.

Gloria heard about the report only through the grapevine. She didn't actually see it, so she didn't know exactly what was in it. In particular, she didn't know if the report attacked her work, expertise, attitude, or anything else. There was good reason to believe it might. After all, if Mr. Mortgage was proposing a reorganization that had room for only one divisional manager, Gloria might reasonably suppose that he would want to be it. This would mean he would have to attack her, either outright or inferentially.

Gloria's question was, what should she do now? She used Game Theory to answer it. She was playing defense in this game. Mr. Mortgage had already made his offensive move, and Gloria had to respond. She figured she had several options:

- She could do nothing, just hunker down and hope for the best.

- She could attack Mr. Mortgage's record.

- She could defend her own work and record.

- She could defend the present two-divisional set-up of the customer service department.

- She could defend both her own work and the present organization.

By using Game Theory's Basic Decision-making Principle, Gloria was able to throw away several of these options right away:

"If I do nothing, what I don't want but am afraid I might get is that the general manager will contrast my lack of attention with Mr. Mortgage's written report. This is no time to look as if you're doing nothing. So this option is out.

"If I attack Mr. Mortgage, what I don't want but am afraid I might get is to make him the sympathetic underdog. Of course, if the general manager knew that I knew Mr. Mortgage had attacked me, that would be one thing. Attacking him would simply be a legitimate way to defend myself. But I don't know what he has done. If he hasn't attacked me, I'll look vicious. So this is a lousy option, too. I won't use it.

"If I simply defend my own work and record, what I don't want but am afraid I might get is that I'll look defensive about it, appear that I have doubts in my own mind about it. And if I have doubts, why shouldn't the general manager? So this option's no good, too.

"If I defend only the present organization, which I believe is the best structure even during hard times, what I don't want but am afraid I might get is that Mr. Mortgage has attacked my work personally. I'll have defended the structure but not myself. This might make it look as if I feel my own work isn't that defensible, as if I am trying to call attention away from it by pointing someplace else. I know my work is good, but the general manager may not. So this is bad, but better than the other options.

"But if I defend both my work and the present structure, what I don't want but am afraid I might get is that Mr. Mortgage will not have attacked my work, only the present divisional structure. Then I might look defensive. Again, this would be bad, but better than my first three options."

So the whole thing hinges on whether or not Mr. Mortgage has attacked your work?

"Yes, and that is precisely what I don't know."

You have decided to defend the present organizational structure, and the only question is whether or not also to defend yourself. Which is worse, defending yourself when he has not attacked or not defending yourself when he has?

"Not defending myself when he has attacked. That's a little worse. So my best strategy is to defend both myself and the present structure. And if he hasn't attacked me, the general manager might figure that I'm merely being thorough rather than defensive."

The interesting point about this kind of defensive situation is that it is not really circular. Why not? The attacker, Mr. Mortgage in this example, has already moved. You don't have to keep anything secret from him. You can simply use your best strategy in your own defense.

Gloria did not wait to be informed of the details of Mr. Mortgage's report. This would have amounted to using the strategy of hunkering down and doing nothing. By the time she found out the game could have been over, with the score, Mr. Mortgage 1, Gloria 0. She wrote up and sent in the report her strategy dictated. A defensive move can be made at any time. You don't have to wait to be informed of the attack.

Incidentally, Gloria got hold of Mr. Mortgage's report about a month after she had sent in her own defensive one. He attacked only the organizational structure, not Gloria. He was both a gentleman and a fool. He suggested a reorganization without at the same time giving very good reasons why he and not his rival should be at the head of it. If you're going to attack, you're a fool if you don't go in for the kill. Otherwise you leave yourself vulnerable to a counterattack from a wounded rival.

These are the lessons from Game Theory in this kind of situation:

- **Find out if you have a rival by examining the present organizational chart and comparing it with the way things used to be. If you are in a parallel position with someone in another division, find out if the two divisions were originally one division.**

- **Find out who this rival is, how desperate he may be.**

- **Listen to the messages coming over the grapevine. Your rival may already have attacked. Incidentally, if he hasn't, you could strike the first blow. The first blow doesn't have to be aggressive.**

- **If you are acting after the attacker has moved, the situation cannot be circular because there is nothing for you to hide from him. You can simply use your best strategy based on the Basic Decision-making Principle of Game Theory.**

24

Dueling over Control of Key Projects—Changing the Situation by Anticipating What It Is Likely to Be

VIRTUALLY ALL DRIVERS CARRY liability and collision insurance, but not many of us want collisions, even if we know we'll collect plenty later. Better to avoid the pain, hassle, unpleasantness, waste of time, and uncertainty. Why don't we do the same thing with office politics and avoid the duels? The best strategists usually do. They change the situation by anticipating what it is likely to be. Game Theory can be tremendously helpful for doing this. It allows you to size up the situation, to see what your chances are. This helps to point you in more imaginative directions, where the hidden sure things can be found.

An example of this occurred at a California Mega-Bank. James, thirty-four, senior V.P. for international credit, with a reputation for ruthlessness, was proposing a major decentralization. His plan contained two elements:

- Regional credit staffs would have the authority to approve exposures up to $6 million. (The existing arrangements limited the regional exposure authority to $4 million. More than that had to be approved at Mega's headquarters.)

- The regional credit staffs wouldn't be under the credit division anymore, but would instead report to the international credit division, i.e., to James.

In short, James was making a power grab. This put him on a collision course with the senior V.P. of the credit division, Monty, fifty, a gracious, generous, and helpful patrician gentleman, whose power would be considerably reduced if the proposed plan were implemented. The irony is that Monty, who tended to give everybody the benefit of the doubt, had helped James get to his present position after James had sought his advice and friendship. Monty had been with the bank a good ten years longer than James and was widely respected by top management. A key meeting of the executive board was scheduled in a week, and Monty considered making his stand at that time. He decided he had three options:

- Attack both aspects of the proposal.

- Attack only the new exposure limits.

- Attack only the new reorganizational aspects of the proposal.

Monty analyzed these options using the Basic Decision-making Principle of Game Theory:

"If I attack both aspects of the plan, what I don't want but am afraid I might get is to be viewed as an obstructionist. This would be very bad.

"If I attack the new exposure limits, what I don't want but am afraid I might get is to place myself as an obstacle in the path of inevitability. Those new credit limits are coming anyway, with or without the new reorganization. So this would be a bad strategy, too.

"If I attack the reorganization, which is the part of the plan I really do object to, what I don't want but am afraid I might get is that James will mount a really strong defense. He might win. This is what I should do, but I don't like it—too chancy."

Monty's best strategy was to attack the reorganization, but he couldn't figure out whether or not he would win the showdown. Game Theory showed him that he was about to be in a collision with an uncertain outcome.

He applied the Basic Decision-making Principle of Game Theory to the entire game: If I play this game, what is it that I don't want but am afraid I might get? The answer was perfectly clear—he might lose. He decided that he'd better not play this game at all. But how to avoid it? He had two obvious strategies:

- He could endorse the reorganization.

- He could propose his own reorganization.

Monty applied the Basic Decision-making Principle to these new strategies:

"If I endorse the plan, what I don't want but am afraid I might get is that I won't head the powerful division. This would be bad.

"If I propose my own plan, what I don't want but am afraid I might get is that it would be laughed out of the boardroom. That would be catastrophic, and also likely, since I don't have another plan at this moment, and anything I came up with on short notice would probably look cooked up. So this choice is out."

Monty now only had to figure out how to head the more powerful new international credit division. This would mean sticking it to James. The obvious question was, in what way was James vulnerable? Monty applied the Basic Decision-making Principle of Game Theory, but this time to James: If James was proposed to head the expanded division, what was it he didn't want but was afraid he might get? Again the answer was obvious. James did not want to be accused of being too inexperienced for the additional responsibilities. If the same question had been asked of Monty, the answer might have been that he didn't want to be accused of being too old. Monty now had his strategy and went in for the kill.

He went to the CEO and endorsed the new reorganization, but suggested that he rather than James should head the much larger international credit division: "James shows tremendous promise, but it's a little risky to give him quite this much responsibility at his age. He's a good 'idea man,' but implementation requires maturity and judgment. Mega has a lot at stake here."

The CEO agreed, and James now works for Monty, who heads the expanded division. The entire issue was resolved before the executive committee meeting, where it was announced, to the astonishment of James.

There are several lessons from Game Theory in this example:

- **Although you can use the Basic Decision-making Principle of Game Theory to evaluate your choices, you still may not be able to predict who will win the showdown.**

- **Just because a showdown is coming doesn't mean you have to participate in it.**

- **If you decide not to fight, you should evaluate your other strengths to see if you can change the nature of the fight. In other words, don't try to fix it, change it into something else, something that you are more confident you can win.**

25

When You Are Caught in the No Man's Land of High Principle

MAKING SURE YOU'RE ON the winning side in a power struggle is generally preferred to the alternative. Of course, there are exceptions, for example, when questions of principle are at issue. But the exceptions are rare; in most office politics cases, if we are really concerned about principle, we wouldn't have anything to do with either side in the dispute. Those who endlessly harp about principle usually fit neatly into one of three categories:

1. Those who have no power and so can't abuse it.
2. Those who have a lot of power and abuse it.
3. Those who are *paid* to talk about it.

The rest of us just try to get through the day. But sometimes we get caught up in the cross fire between groups or individuals who espouse high-sounding principles. Game Theory can be enormously helpful in figuring out what to do when you are caught in the middle of this kind of high-principled duel.

This situation confronts Pat, the day manager at a very large Philadelphia restaurant. Pat got the job six months ago, after two years as a waiter at the place. In addition to being day manager, he is still a waiter on the dinner shift. So Pat is both lower management and blue collar. This is a peculiar position, since he has torn loyalties—to his fellow waiters, and to management, which can advance his career. Actually, the management of the restaurant thinks he is an extraordinary waiter, and the rest of the waiters like him, too, so when he was promoted everyone was happy.

Except Frankie, who felt passed over. Frankie is second in seniority and never lets anyone forget it. Not that he ever had a prayer of getting the job. Management hates him because he infuriates everyone—the other waiters, the bartenders, the chefs and kitchen staff, let alone the maître d', the manager, and the owners. Why doesn't the manager just fire the guy? The waiters are unionized, and the rules for dismissal are quite specific. Management has to show cause, a vague term that includes several possible offenses:

- **Chronic lateness**—Frankie is the most punctual guy there.

- **Stealing**—Frankie doesn't.

- **Drunkenness**—Frankie is a teetotaler.

- **Serving "untouched" rolls and butter left over from one customer to the next one**—management encourages everyone to do this during rush periods, despite its violation of local laws.

As you might suspect, Frankie is nailed by management for violating the last "rule": re-serving the "untouched" rolls and butter. Of course, the union can't let this pass—if Frankie is fired for it, every other waiter in the joint could be, too. This, however, isn't the reason the union publicly gives out, since it incriminates the rest of its members. The public reason is that management has no evidence to support its admittedly horrifying accusations. And management isn't about to rehire this guy; because they hate him, they want to show the other waiters who the boss is, and they have to defend the principle that The Law mustn't be violated. Frankie files a grievance and the two sides find themselves, under the terms of their labor-management contract, in binding arbitration.

How does Pat get caught up in this duel? He's the star witness, for both sides. That's right, each side calls him as their principal witness. Because of Pat's unique position of both full-time waiter and day manager, each side is convinced he's in their pocket. Pat's problem is, what should he do?

He needs Game Theory badly and uses it to sort out his problem. He decides he has three choices:

- Back up management by testifying to whatever they want to hear.

- Back up Frankie by testifying to whatever the union wants to hear.

- Try not to back up anybody, but act as dumb as he can.

Pat analyzes his options using the Basic Decision-making Principle of Game Theory:

"If I back up Frankie, what I don't want but am sure I will get is that I can kiss my career at this restaurant goodbye. So this option is out.

"On the other hand, if I back up management, what I don't want but am afraid I might get is that the arbitrator might decide for Frankie. Then I'll be branded not only as a traitor but as an unsuccessful one. The rest of the waiters will probably kick up a fuss if I'm kept on as day manager, so I'd probably be demoted.

"If I try to avoid giving any information away during my testimony, what I don't want but am afraid I might get is that Frankie will lose, and I'll feel like a rat for not saying that everybody, including me, does what Frankie is being fired for. That would be lousy, but I guess it's my best strategy. . . . Maybe I'll be lucky and the arbitrator will find for Frankie."

The arbitrator rules in favor of the restaurant, but Pat, who is still the day manager, doesn't feel too bad about it. Neither side's attorneys ask the one pertinent question: Does management recommend or condone the practice of re-serving "untouched" rolls and butter? Why don't they ask the main point? Management doesn't want to admit to conspiring to break the law. And the union doesn't want to admit that all of its members (at this restaurant, anyway) are doing it, too—they could all be fired.

There is one lesson that Game Theory teaches from this example:

- **If you're caught in the middle of a duel over principle between two high-sounding sides, protect yourself.**

26

When You Know You Can't Win

WHO WANTS TO HEAR in advance that he's going to get his rear kicked? You do, if you want to avoid it. Game Theory can show you if you'll lose, providing you aren't up against a half-wit.

On the other hand, have you ever noticed how truly intelligent half-wits are these days, especially the ones in upper management? They can be so intelligent that they can provoke you into a foolish, impromptu, disastrous action, such as telling them what you really think of them. Game Theory can be a great help in detecting set-ups. There still may be no way you can win, your job may be over no matter what you do, but it may make some difference to you in the future precisely how you make your exit.

This was the situation confronting Ed, the assistant controller at a major New York advertising agency. His boss, Tony,

wanted him out, but he didn't want to come out and say it because the problem was one of personality. They hated each
other. This was not viewed as a good enough reason to can
somebody, so his boss tried to set him up. He sent a memo out-
lining a new staff position, to report directly to him. The president would have to okay the change.

This was the key to Tony's scheme. He was hoping that Ed,
in a fit of rage, would go to the president to protest. Over the
years Ed had gone around Tony to the president quite a few
times, and Tony anticipated that he would do it again. What Ed
didn't know was that Tony had already primed the president to
expect Ed's visit and had already rebutted most of the arguments
Ed might use.

What Tony did not know is that Ed knew Game Theory and,
before saying anything, worked through his options and his
long-term prospects at the agency. He decided that both were
limited and that he had better find a job somewhere else. To do
this would require a few months, so he geared his strategy to
that objective. He decided he had to respond to the new plan.
This left him with two options:

- Oppose the new staff position.

- Endorse the new position, but fault it in detail, such as
  the fact that the new position would report directly to
  the controller. It could even more legitimately be set up
  to report to the assistant controller, Ed.

Ed evaluated his options using the Basic Decision-making
Principle of Game Theory:

"If I oppose the new staff position, what I don't want but
am afraid I might get is that I'll be overruled. This will create an
awkward situation, and the awkward situation could be used as
the legitimate excuse for firing me. So this is bad.

"If I endorse the new position but suggest modification,
such as having the new guy report to me, what I don't want but
am afraid I might get is that they'll go along with my suggestion.

Then I'll have some new schnook to train, but this would buy me time while I quietly look for another job. And if they turn down my suggestion, I'll still have endorsed the basic plan, so the situation won't be really awkward. They'll have to find some other reason to fire me, which again gives me time."

Ed arranged a meeting with the president and Tony in the president's office. They were geared up to rebut Ed's objections. He never made them, but instead suggested the modification of the plan. This threw the other two off guard and bought Ed three more months on the job. He's now a controller at another agency.

There are several lessons from Game Theory in this kind of example:

- **Game Theory may show there is no way you can win this game.**

- **The analysis may reveal a hidden trap, a set-up. Often no-win situations are designed for provocation rather than anything else.**

- **You don't have to take the bait. You can use a nonprovocative strategy. Often this requires some sort of endorsement of what you oppose. But this will buy you time.**

Part 3
Trapping

27

The Conqueror's Racket— Keeping You on Your Toes Instead of on His

ALL OF THE DUELS we have looked at share a common property— whatever one guy wins the other loses. Sometimes they're battling over a free trip to Acapulco, at other times over who controls key projects. But the main thing is, two persons are scrambling over something, almost always while somebody else watches.

Regardless of who wins the scramble, the person who keeps score always win. You pay him in one of two ways, and sometimes both. One way is to increase his productivity by killing yourself to outshine some other sucker. A second way is to so exhaust yourself slugging it out with the other guy that you don't have time or energy to threaten the third party who got you into the fight in the first place. If he's got two guys trying to slit each other's throats, they're too desperate to gang up against him. Whoever has set up this deal is using the conqueror's racket of keeping the subject people divided among themselves. You don't need the Roman Empire to understand this. It happens every day at your office. You've been trapped.

Of course, setting traps doesn't always work to management's advantage. Sometimes the big shots succeed in trapping themselves. Somebody still collects a commission, almost always a lawyer, but that's incidental to the main action, which is the self-inflicted trap-wound.

A particularly notorious example of this was the Bendix/Martin Marietta takeover fight. Bill Agee, head of Bendix, tried to take over Martin Marietta in an unfriendly bid. Top management at Marietta thought otherwise, so they took out a huge loan and simultaneously took over Bendix. The two companies ended up taking each other over, and the lawyers made a bundle sorting it out. As I said, somebody always collects a commission in a trapping situation.

This was an example of the Prisoner's Dilemma game. The name comes from a situation in which a district attorney has two prisoners whom he is certain committed a crime together, but he lacks proof. However, he has a plan to get it. He puts the two suspects in separate rooms and gives each one a chance to turn state's evidence on the other. This is what happens under the different possibilities:

- If one rats and the other keeps his mouth shut, the one who fingers gets off free. The one who is loyally silent takes the full rap.

- If both confess, they both get sent up, but for less than the maximum because they cooperated with the cops.

- If both keep their lips buttoned, they both get put out on the street again, after a couple of unpleasant days with a rubber hose, because the cops have no proof.

Each crook looks at this problem and says to himself: "I better squeal, otherwise he might, and I'll spend the rest of my life in the slammer." So they both confess and both spend ten years in prison. Actually this trap doesn't always work with common criminals, but as we have seen, it sometimes does with corporation presidents.

Watch Out for Your Own Well-meaning Booby Traps!

The Prisoner's Dilemma trap is one of the easiest to set amateurishly, and then blunder into oneself. Many a manager has set

this trap himself, only to fall into it later. The result is that he has
been stymied by his superiors, who thought him insensitive to
the needs of his subordinates. The superiors, of course, couldn't
care less about the so-called needs of the middle manager's subordinates. But good underlings are hard to find, and the superiors don't want to put themselves in a spot where their own peers
or superiors bend their ears about the middle manager's insensi-
tivity and stupidity in losing them. If the big shots really were
worried about the poor tormented flunkies, the higher-ups
would summarily fire the insensitive middle manager and send
all the bruised underlings on expense-paid vacations to the Baha-
mas.

The trick is to avoid unwittingly setting up amateurish Prisoner's Dilemmas that backfire in your face. Here are the key elements of this particular trap:

- The "prisoners," i.e., your subordinates:

  * don't trust each other

  * or don't like each other

  * or don't talk to each other.

- You set up a situation in which each one thinks he has a
  chance to come out personally way ahead by screwing
  the others, who end up absolutely devastated, lost beyond hope.

- If they each try to push the others out of the lifeboat,
  they all end up in the drink, but still clinging to the side
  of the now capsized boat.

- If they don't go for each other's throats, there is something in it for them, but not much.

These rules are the basic structure of any panic situation, including stock market panics and arms races, but only of *some* office
politics dilemmas.

To illustrate the dangers inherent in their naive application,

we'll look at an example. Barry, the director of a computer training school in the Midwest, planned to use them for a noble purpose. He planned to trap a couple of feuding employees into
cooperating despite themselves.

The sales manager, Jack, and the operations manager,
Quentin, don't get along. In fact, one would be hard-pressed
to determine which detests the other more. The big season for
the school was coming up, and both Jack and Quentin needed
clerical assistants. Unfortunately, because of demographic
changes in the area, enrollment was down at the school. Barry
would have liked to hire two assistants but had the money to
hire only one. He therefore came up with an absolutely fair,
even Solomonesque solution. He would hire the best assistant
available, and the two managers could split his time evenly
between them.

Barry was totally on top of his job and knew that the two
managers hated each other. To prevent either one from deliberately hogging all the assistant's time, Barry called in each of them
separately—he was tired that day and didn't want to hear them
squabble with each other—to tell them in no uncertain terms:
"If I see you aren't using the assistant's time productively, I'll
give him to the other manager full-time."

Barry thought he was being an effective manager. In fact, he
practically ruined his career by deliberately, but amateurishly,
setting up a vicious Prisoner's Dilemma between Jack and Quentin. Unfortunately for Barry, they spotted the trap, and Barry
was the one who got caught in it. He ended up being blamed by
the school's president for incompetent management.

This is what happened: Barry interviewed a series of incompetent potential assistants until he finally found one who just
might do—Buzz. Jack and Quentin assessed him as adequate, if
just barely so.

Quentin and Jack were called in separately to Barry's office and asked if they wanted to hire Buzz. Each responded,
"no," to Barry's shock. How come? They both reasoned the
same way:

"If I say hire this guy, with the aim of getting his exclusive use, what I don't want but am afraid I might get is that the other manager will also say 'hire him.' Then I have to work with that idiot by coordinating the use of Buzz.

"If I say don't hire him, what I don't want but am afraid I might get is that the other manager will urge that he be hired. Then the other manager gets full use of the assistant and I'm left on my own, which is worse."

So far, a standard Prisoner's Dilemma. Even two half-wits should choose to "hire Buzz" to end up splitting his time down the middle. This is what Barry had been counting on. But wait a minute, there was a twist. Neither Jack nor Quentin was a half-wit. Each of them, on his own, carried the reasoning one step further:

"That jackass Barry thinks he can trick us into doing what he wants by pretending he's the D.A. interrogating a couple of mugs. To hell with him, and to hell with Buzz."

Buzz wasn't hired, and the two managers spent the busy season without adequate assistance. Barry was criticized by the president of the school for recklessly overworking key staff: "How are we going to hold them if you treat them like this?"

He tried to cover by dishonestly claiming he was using the Prisoner's Dilemma backhandedly to hold down expenses. But this flimflam didn't wash when the president, a former union member, said: "Don't take me for a fool. Don't you think I know that emotional solidarity will beat heartless logic every time?"

The lesson from Game Theory in this example is very clear:

- **The Prisoner's Dilemma can be foiled by implicit peer solidarity.**

28

The Speed Trap

HAVE YOU EVER SEEN a gladiator movie on late-night TV? If so, you've seen a standard scene, which appears in virtually all such movies, as any fellow insomniac can testify. The scene is this: A gladiator armed with a broadsword goes up against another one armed with a net and pitchfork. This scene has inspired countless work reorganizations at corporations across the country.

They inevitably go under the name "team projects," "team assignments," or "team *something*." The word "team" is always in there someplace, to put a smile on a situation that calls for a frown. Our minds might picture the football team, the baseball team, the basketball team, but what the phrase is really referring to is the gladiator team, the dueling team, the chain-gang team, and the kamikaze team.

Is it fair to blame your boss for instituting these team projects? Is he the one who is *really* responsible? Or is he simply under the gun, too, forced to deliver to his boss, who in turn must look good to his own boss? After all, your boss isn't a monster but another human being with a soul and feelings. If you cut him he'll bleed. Don't cut him. Use Game Theory to figure out a better strategy.

Henry got trapped in a team project. He had worked for a year and a half as an internal auditor in a cable television company in the Southwest. The standard auditing method was to assign one auditor per audit. This is the way it had always been done at the company—until Henry's boss suggested a "scientific" experiment to top management. The experiment was simply to assign two auditors to the same project. The test was to see if this would speed up the work or slow it down, increase the quality of the report, or decrease it. Obviously it would "speed it up" in one sense. If there were no new obstacles—such as personality clashes between the team members—the audit should be finished in half the usual time. But this would not constitute a real speed-up since the same number of man-hours would perform the same amount of work. A speed-up could occur only if the audit were done in less than half the usual time. This is what the test would show.

So far, there are no elements of broadsword against fishnet, but the manager created them. He paired two auditors with vastly different strengths. Although both were thought to be highly accurate, Henry was considered by management to be extremely speedy with the audit itself, but also extremely abrupt in writing it up into a report. The gentleman he was teamed up with, Rick, was considered by management to move at a snail's pace in performing the actual audit, but what a report writer! There we have it, broadsword against fishnet—except for the competitive elements. On the contrary, the two auditors should have complemented each other perfectly, especially since they liked each other. Here was the trap: The manager would look over the results of the audit and award a single promotion to the one team member who appeared to do the best job. If they both appeared to do equally well, they would split a bonus equally and neither would get the promotion.

What if they both did a lousy job? The manager might feel that he had to fire both auditors. He had proposed this scheme to top management, and if it didn't work, he'd have to blame it on somebody. So our two auditor-gladiators couldn't get together to hold back.

Even without this threat, they couldn't get together, because the manager had constructed a very efficient trap. To see this, consider Henry's and Rick's options:

Henry's options:

- He could blast the audit out as fast as humanly possible.

- He could finish the audit at his usual pace.

- He could sit on his calculator, bringing the audit in late.

Rick's options:

- He could go for the Pulitzer Prize in accounting.

- He could write his usual workmanlike prose.

- He could write a report that would be rejected as unreadable even by the editor of the worst management textbook in the United States.

Henry evaluated his strategies using the Basic Decision-making Principle of Game Theory:

"If I go slow, what I don't want but am afraid I might get is that Rick will write at least the usual, and maybe a superb report. Then I'm screwed.

"The same thing goes if I simply bring in the audit at the usual pace. Rick has the chance to shine, and I could be ruined.

"My only rational strategy is to bring in the audit at the speed of an electronic calculator. What I don't want but am afraid I might get then is that Rick will write a superb report, and we'll split the bonus, with no promotion."

A similar line of reasoning, had Rick done it, would have resulted in Rick's writing a superb report. But Rick was neither gladiator nor game strategist. He wrote his usual report, and the broadsword triumphed.

Henry got the promotion—to another department, away from his former boss, the audit manager, with whom he has not been very friendly since. Rick? He left the company a few months later.

What could Henry have done in retaliation to the audit manager? Nothing, absolutely nothing. The company is organized in this way, and there is no justice in it. Henry simply had to accept that fact.

The great advantage of Game Theory in this kind of situation is that it tells you the depth of the trap you are in, and shows that the only way you can get out is to kill the innocent. That's what the gladiators had to do, too.

This discussion leads us to the Fifth Corollary to the Basic Decision-making Principle of Game Theory:

Almost all office traps can be avoided, and in the few that can't be, you always stand at least a fighting chance.

29

Entrapment and the Light at the End of the Tunnel

IT'S RUSH HOUR AND there aren't any taxis. If you run, you can just make it—sweaty, tired, and angry. On the other hand, if you wait for the bus or subway, and it comes on time, you'll be delivered to your appointment with ease. What do you do, take the bus or make a run for it?

You've been dialing for what seems like hours, always getting a busy signal, when finally the person answers. You speak for a few seconds, but just before you get the key information across, the person puts you on hold. And you wait and wait and wait. What do you do, hang up and try later, or hang on and go crazy?

You've driven around looking for a parking space and at last you find one. You pull up parallel to the car ahead, to get ready to back in, when some swine in a small car zips into your space.

Do you stay and argue, or drive away and look for another space?

These are entrapments. They are excruciatingly frustrating, and hideously common. Game Theory can help to remove them from your business life.

Here are the characteristics of entrapments:

- You view your time, money, energy, or pride as an investment, a sunk cost, in the activity.

- As more of this item is invested, you think you're getting closer to your goal, but the cost is running up, too.

- You're tempted to hang in because you think you're getting closer to your goal, and because you'll have to write off the whole investment of time, money, energy, or pride if you give up.

Julie was trapped in an office politics version of this. She had read some futurology books and bought the arguments. The American economy, she had decided, is going to be more and more "information intensive" and "high tech." She came to the decision that personal computers are the wave of the future, so she decided to get into that business. This sounds like a perfectly reasonable idea, but Julie didn't know her byte from her floppy disk.

No matter, she had been in sales in cosmetics, so she figured she'd go into sales in personal computers and get on-the-job training on the technical stuff. Again, not a bad plan. She made the move about six months ago, getting a job as a customer service representative for the only Chicago office of a computer company headquartered in California. The company produces a line of portable personal computers—quite good ones, as it turns out. Why would a high-tech company hire somebody who doesn't have one single bit of knowledge about computers? That's always been the computer business.

This, however, brought up her problem. She had to rely on people who really knew computers, and the one she had to consult the most was an exceptionally unpleasant guy named Chuck. He was obsessed by computers and brilliant with them, but as is often the case with those obsessed, short on any social graces. He was incoherently technical, impatient with those who didn't instantly understand his instructions, and a nerd to boot.

To sell to potential customers meant demonstrating the machine and the software that runs on it. This required that Julie talk to Chuck. She had to answer technical questions for the customers and provide follow-up support—both of which required Chuck's help.

In short, there was no way she could avoid Chuck. But each time she went to him for information, he rubbed her face in the dirt before supplying her with the answer. However, she did get the information, so she felt that she was getting a little closer to gaining the needed technical knowledge.

But a flaw in her understanding of the high-tech world and her previous experience in cosmetics left her totally unprepared. In cosmetics, one had to learn the business only once. But in the field of personal computers, the amount of knowledge necessary to really know the field keeps increasing. Unless one has an intuitive feel for the subject, one can be in a real jam passing oneself off as an expert. Sure, any of us can learn word processing or financial analysis with a single personal computer. But what about making a sale when your company puts out a new model every three weeks and introduces new and often very sophisticated software every week? The light at the end of the tunnel never seems to get any closer, and maybe even slips a little farther away. In short, there always seemed to be a Chuck in Julie's future.

Julie was caught inside a microprocessor. It had all the elements of an entrapment: Time and energy were sunk into a project the goal of which was always out of reach. Julie used Game Theory to sort it out. She decided she had three options:

- stay the course

- go back to the cosmetics business

- try to switch to another personal computer company.

She evaluated each of her options using the Basic Decision-making Principle of Game Theory:

"If I stay the course, what I don't want but am afraid I might get is that I'll always be dependent on someone like Chuck. In other words, I'll never achieve the kind of independence I had in the cosmetics business, and I'll always be unhappy, frustrated, and basically unsuccessful. To sell these damn things, you have to be able to really demonstrate them. That's the problem.

"If I change jobs, this means I have to go to another computer company, because I'm at the only Chicago office of my company. So, for openers, I'd have to learn a whole new system—start all over again. What I don't want but am afraid I might get is another Chuck. I've heard that there are a lot of guys like Chuck in this industry. This would be the absolute worst.

"If I go back to the cosmetics business, what I don't want but am afraid I might get, in fact what I will get, is to lose everything I've put into personal computers—all the time, energy, torture, and awfulness of dealing with Chuck. The question is, is losing my investment in Chuck worse than putting an even bigger investment in that jerk? The answer is obviously no, putting more time into Chuck is obviously worse. Besides, I already know the cosmetics business."

Game Theory helped Julie come to understand why she should cut her losses and go back to a business where she didn't have to run like hell just to stay in place. She got a job not with her old cosmetics company but with another one, which was instituting a new personal computer system for its various marketing departments. They hired her because of her presumed expertise in computers. In fact, by this time she did know more than most of the people there about personal computers. By the way, her new company bought the computers manufactured by her old company, and Julie was once again in contact with Chuck.

These are the lessons from Game Theory in entrapments:

- **Recognize the key elements of an entrapment:**
  * **Your time, energy, money, or pride has been sunk into a project.**
  * **The goal continues to elude you while the costs keep going up.**
  * **If you cut your losses, you have to abandon your investment.**
- **Apply the Basic Decision-making Principle of Game Theory. By focusing on what you don't want but are afraid you might get, you can escape the trap. You are caught in the trap only because the objective keeps luring you into it. The moment you look at the trap instead of the goal, you can free yourself.**

30

Macho Traps

A MOVIE DIRECTOR TOLD me the story of the Macho Trap: After much struggle a brilliant woman writer/producer got her totally original detective story series on the air during prime time. But it was canceled after thirteen weeks. Bum ratings? Sure, but the audience was building. Another few weeks and it would have been a contender. Then why did the network cancel it? Because of a power struggle with the independent production company.

The independent company had a great deal of control over the project because they had assumed some of the financial risk from the network. But to get the show done in a way that would

allow it to find its own audience, the woman had confronted
key executives at the independent. They got very "macho" and
tried to get her to back down on several major plot elements. She
wouldn't budge, figuring they would have to give in or lose the
show, including all of their investment and very real prospects
of very big money, especially from some exceedingly profitable
syndication deals. The independent producers wouldn't budge
either, and the whole package went over the cliff.

She could have compromised by folding on an issue or two.
And she should have known better. In college, she wrote her senior thesis on James Dean's most famous movie, *Rebel Without
a Cause.* In the big scene, James Dean and the leading high-
school juvenile delinquent play chicken: They race stolen cars
toward a cliff, and the first one to jump is labeled "chicken."
The brave one gets Natalie Wood.

Why did our writer/producer fall into the trap? She thought
if she played with the big boys she would have to act like them,
too. This was her mistake. She forgot that although both may go
over the cliff, the senior producer just might have a safety net.
He had a lot of shows in the works, so it would take more than
one trashed show to knock him off the tube.

Here are the rules for the Macho Game of Chicken:

- There has to be an outcome that is only pretty good for
  both parties. Some call this the cooperative outcome,
  others call it the panty-waisted one.

- If both players go for the panty-waisted outcome, either
  one can do better by switching his strategy to macho.
  That guy looks strong and macho while the other one
  looks weak and panty-waisted.

- If they both go for macho, they both get ruined. This is
  the worst for both of them, and for either one it is worse
  than being panty-waisted when the other one is macho.

Let's look at another example of a Macho Trap, this one
from banking. Sid was the CEO of Big Moo Moo, a major Florida

dress manufacturer. He had been the boss there since 1960, when the board of directors hired him away from the investment banking company that Big Moo Moo had been dealing with. Sid had handled the Big Moo Moo account for the bank, and the board of directors was obviously very impressed.

Sid was amazingly successful at Big Moo Moo. He was only forty-one when he started there and was generally credited with single-handedly keeping the company profitable for over twenty years. In the course of this time, he diversified into a number of related products. His cozy relationship with his old bank made the financing of these acquisitions relatively easy and always successful. Problems came up, as they inevitably do, but they were handled in a spirit of full cooperation, with nobody wanting to win at anybody else's expense. However, the years passed, and his old cronies at the bank passed with them.

The new man on the account was Reginald, a thirty-year-old Harvard MBA. Sid, not a man to mince words, described Reginald as a "horse's ass." Still, they did business together although they weren't exactly pals, as was the case with Sid and the bankers in the old days. Under no circumstances would Sid have played chicken with the old bankers, and vice versa—they were pals and colleagues.

Reginald objected to one of Sid's plans for refinancing the debt of a small retail chain he had recently acquired. Reginald insisted on two conditions before the $15 million in short-term credit would be issued:

- Sid had to get Reginald's okay before making any new acquisitions.
- Big Moo Moo would issue five-year bonds for $40 million.

The interesting thing is that in the old days, Sid wouldn't have dreamed of making an acquisition without bending the ears of his cronies at the bank about it. He'd go on about it so long they'd sometimes virtually hang up on him, saying, "So buy already!" And as for the long-term bond issue, Sid had planned to suggest the identical idea to Reginald, but Reginald had beat him to it. In the old days, Sid and his banking cronies used to compete to see who could come up with the best financing plan. But when Reginald presented these two issues as demands, Sid nearly punched his face in.

He couldn't bring himself to back down, he hated Reginald so much. The result was a rapid deterioration of Big Moo Moo. As a result of this, Reginald was fired from the bank, and what's left of Big Moo Moo now banks elsewhere.

Why is an otherwise intelligent business person dumb enough to be macho, to play chicken? There is no shortage of answers, all of them good as far as they go. The anthropologist will tell us that this is a cultural question: In England, displaying macho behavior is considered very poor taste and very low class. A sociologist might say that this is how social dominance is established. A psychologist might say that this is a manifestation of an unresolved Oedipal complex. A biologist might say something about too many Y chromosomes. However, from our standpoint the question is not why boys will be boys, but whether or not one has to play, and if so, how to beat the other guy at it.

The answer to the first part of the question is obvious: You don't have to play. But to avoid playing you must establish a dialogue based on friendship and communality. This is what Sid had going for him with his old cronies.

If you have to play chicken, you can beat the guy who is macho in one of two ways. One is to try to match his macho, so maybe he'll back down, or maybe you'll both go over the cliff. This way isn't a sure thing. The other way is to lose. Lose? Right, lose. This is the ancient method of feminine wiles. Let him win. Let him be macho. He gets the macho, you get the money. After he's won, don't play chicken with him anymore. Turn the game into something else by befriending the macho man. Make him not want to compete with you. Make him want to give you things. This sounds manipulative? Of course it's manipulative! What would you rather do, drive over a cliff?

Part 4
Muscling

31

Figuring Out If You Can Muscle

ALL OF THE EXAMPLES in this section will deal with situations in which persons either deliberately do various kinds of harm or threaten to do so. Wasn't this also true for all of our games in Part II on Dueling? Yes, but there are significant differences.

Dueling:

- Whatever one guy wins the other one loses. They both cannot win at the same time.

- Threats play no meaningful role. Why should they? The two guys are already at each other's throats.

Muscling:

- Both may win or both may lose at the same time. Or one guy might lose more than the other wins.

- Threats can play a very big role, as one may try to menace the other into doing something that is not obviously to the menaced person's advantage.

If you are muscling someone, or being muscled yourself, you should keep in mind *how vulnerable* you and the other guy are. Game Theory can be very helpful in establishing these points, as shown in the following example:

Lynn, thirty-one, was faced with a problem of evaluating

mutual vulnerability on her job. She had recently been promoted
to director of marketing incentives at a large home appliances
and consumer products manufacturing company in Toronto.
Her first assignment was to set up a trip to Cancun, Mexico, for
the top five hundred salespersons.

Virtually every big company has a travel department to arrange for executive business trips. For reasons that Lynn could
never find out, and still doesn't know, she was told to arrange
this trip through a specific outside travel agency. In fact, the trip
to Cancun was the only trip of any kind at the company which
was not arranged through the in-house travel department.

This trip was not exactly small change. Each of the five hundred could bring a spouse—so we're really talking about one
thousand travelers, each of them going Mega-First Class. "Mega-
First Class" is first class to the point of vulgar, even obscene,
gluttony. The company didn't want to be accused of being cheap
with its top salespersons, and it wasn't. The total bill for the trip
came to over $2 million. Lynn had her suspicions that with a
total bill this big, and the outside travel agent getting at least 10
percent of it, there was a remote possibility of a private arrangement between the senior executive who ordered her to use this
travel agent and the agent. But she could not prove it, nor did
she want to try.

Other than arranging through a travel agent for her own vacation to the Virgin Islands, she knew nothing about travel arrangements. Nor had she had any experience with coordinating
major events across departmental lines at her company. This put
her in a bit of a pickle. If she screwed up, or if any part of the
arrangements got screwed up, whether or not she had anything
to do with it she would be blamed. Her worst nightmares were
of five hundred outraged top supersalespersons all simultaneously descending on the CEO and selling him on the idea of
drowning her in Lake Ontario because they all got *turista* in
Cancun. That things might go wrong was more than a possibility, it was a constant nagging fear, made worse by the fact that

she had no idea what might go wrong. In other words, she did not know whether to describe herself as inexperienced, incompetent, or incompetent due to inexperience.

Her problem was that someone at the company was going around describing her in all three of those ways. Who? Jeannie, the manager of the in-house travel department, who didn't like the fact that the trip was being organized outside her department. She also was curious why this was so, and she also didn't want to investigate. But she did want to do what she could, covertly, to make sure that the trip was a flop. She didn't want any precedents set for successful trips that she had had nothing to do with. There was always a chance that the whole in-house travel department would be phased out, and her job with it. So she felt vulnerable.

Lynn was aware of Jeannie's concern, and so was particularly perplexed when Bert, Lynn's boss, told her to meet with Jeannie to go over the plans for the trip, "just to make sure everything is hunky-dory," as he put it. Of course, Lynn had her suspicions that a great deal about this trip was not "hunky-dory," especially about Bert and his possible kickback arrangement with the outside travel agent.

Lynn figured she could pull off the trip if she could devote her full attention to it. The major distraction she feared was being endlessly hounded by worried executives. The source of their worry would of course be bad-mouth remarks from Jeannie.

Lynn had to figure out how to lock Jeannie into a soundproof compartment. She used Corollary Six to the Basic Principle:

The basic idea of muscling is to lock the other person into a fixed position, where he cannot move without being punished. Then you have to hope he is not a glutton for punishment.

Lynn figured she had two basic strategies:

- She could inform Jeannie of the broad outlines of the trip, but not ask her for any specific recommendations.

- She could request specific pointers on what to do.

Lynn used the Basic Decision-making Principle of Game Theory to assess her own vulnerability:

"If I don't ask for advice, what I don't want but am afraid I might get is no help from her, which isn't so bad, because I don't trust her help anyway. Also, if I just show her the broad outlines of the trip, without any real specifics, she won't be in a position to *credibly* criticize me until the trip is over.

"If I try to get specifics from her, what I don't want but am afraid I might get is her spreading the word that I am incompetent. The project might be taken away from me. So this is worse."

Her best strategy was obviously not to ask for advice, and the application of the Basic Decision-making Principle had revealed to her where she was most vulnerable. However, when using a *muscling strategy* one must do one more thing, which is to apply the Basic Decision-making Principle one more time, to the person you plan to muscle. This is an application of Corollary Seven to the Basic Principle:

You can use the Basic Decision-making Principle of Game Theory to figure out the other person's, as well as your own, vulnerability.

Lynn did this:

"If I tell Jeannie only the broad outlines, what is it that Jeannie doesn't want but is afraid she might get? Excluded from the project? No, she's already excluded. Phased out, if the project is successful? She's afraid of that, but it's long term. Blamed for sabotaging the project with bad advice? That's it! She doesn't want to be blamed for sabotaging it."

So, the day before the arranged meeting Lynn sent a memo to Jeannie, with carbon copies to Bert and to Jeannie's boss:

Jeannie—

Thanks for your interest in the trip to Cancun. I've pretty much completed all the arrangements with the outside travel agency, and I'm looking forward to going over the high points with you at our meeting tomorrow. If you have any suggestions, please set them down in a memo to me, and I'll pass it along to the outside travel agent.

Needless to say, Jeannie had no suggestions, nor was she about to make any comments to anyone about the trip, since Lynn had now gone on record asking that if she was volunteering any comments, they be put in writing. Lynn had successfully sealed Jeannie into a soundproof room. Game Theory had pointed her in the right direction for doing so, by revealing Lynn's vulnerability.

There are several key lessons from Game Theory in situations such as this:

- **Apply the Basic Decision-making Principle of Game Theory to yourself to establish your own vulnerability.**

- **Apply the same principle to the person you want to muscle, to figure out where he is vulnerable.**

- **Use the understanding of vulnerability as a guide to figure out how to lock the other person into the place you want him.**

32

How to Muscle the Guy Who Hangs Out with the Boss

WE HAVE LOOKED AT various ways by which a boss could keep his subordinates at each others' throats and away from his own. An examination of the various possible traps showed that the only surefire one was to catch the subordinates in the trap of a duel. The reason was simple—in a duel, the duelers cannot trust each other long enough to turn around and shoot the referee, so the boss is safe.

But the boss always has the high cards—he sets the rules. What happens when you are not a boss, and your boss is not trying to trap you into anything? Great! What's your problem? *A rival.* Someone is angling for your job, not because your boss has set him up to it but because he's ambitious.

Unlike your boss, you don't have the luxury of making the rules, at least not all of them. Not that that is necessarily such an advantage. We've looked at a lot of examples where bosses had this luxury but fouled up anyway. Besides, there can be another advantage to not having the ability to make the rules: If you don't have it, your rival probably doesn't either. So your problem is simply to figure out what the structure of the situation is and do the best you can within it.

Fortunately, the set-up is often the same, and often perfectly simple. To see this, ask yourself one question: What does the term "office politics" usually mean? Excelling at one's job? Are you kidding? Honest hard work? Come on! Okay, getting the advantage on the other guy by being rewarded for something other than merit. We've certainly seen examples of *that* in this book. So we come to one of the definitions of a political person in the office:

A person is defined as *political* in the context of the office if he spends most of his efforts buttering up the boss.

There are various ways this can be accomplished, and one of the best is through flattery.

But flattery is tricky to pull off. Most people will be suspicious of compliments. If they even suspect they are bad-looking and you tell them they are good-looking, eventually they'll suspect you're a liar. Similarly, if you tell them they're smart when they're pretty sure they're at best dull, you're eventually in for trouble. It'll take a while, because they may believe you for a brief period, but eventually their basic doubts are bound to overcome your superficial remarks.

However, there is one surefire method of flattery that almost never fails—*being around.* This doesn't require that you compliment the person on anything. The simple act of hanging around someone *is* the compliment. He thinks to himself, "Maybe I'm not such a jerk after all if this guy wants to hang around me, if he's willing to give up his time to be around *me.*" This type of flattery is effective precisely because it plays on the insecurities of the person being flattered. All flattery does that, but this type does so in a much more insidious way: It lets the person flatter himself.

Take a good look at the people in your office whom you think are political. Most of them use the strategy of hanging out with the boss. They don't overtly flatter him or offer compliments or bring gifts. They simply hang out with him. You see this going on when your rival goes into the boss's office and you rack your brain to figure out what is going on in there. You might go through bursts of paranoia as you fear that your rival is somehow plotting against you. Later, you find out that he and the boss were talking about the relative merits of different park-

ing lots. Trivia. Your rival wasn't up to anything? Wrong. He
was up to *being with the boss*—and that's plenty.

If you breathe a sigh of relief you shouldn't. Your rival talks
to the boss about trivia, whereas you talk to him about declines
in sales and other weighty and often unpleasant matters. Given a
choice between your rival and you—and your boss has that
choice—whom do you think the boss would prefer to talk to?
You lose just by doing your job.

This chapter will show you how to counter the strategy of
the guy who hangs out. There are several ways, and an analysis
based on Game Theory shows that each has its pitfalls.

Lee was recently in this pickle. He works in the production
department of an Atlanta advertising agency. He has a key job
there, working out the financial nuts and bolts of budgets for TV
commercials. Producers come up with proposed budgets, but
Lee figures out how the agency will actually allot the money.
He's a powerful man, so producers are constantly coming to him
for advice. Lee reports directly to the V.P. of production, who
has a great deal of confidence in his ability.

But the V.P. was having a lot more fun with another guy,
Bo, a financial analyst in the treasurer's office. Because of his
position, Bo knew who was making what. He had seen how
much Lee was making and would have liked to make it himself. To do this, he had to muscle out Lee. There was only one
hitch: Bo had no experience in production. However, he
planned to make up for this minor obstacle by winning the
confidence of the production V.P., and he was doing this by
hanging out with him.

Since it was widely recognized at the agency that Lee was
doing a good job, there was no way in the world Bo could
muscle him out—as things stood. But the organizational structure could soon change, and all three of our characters knew
it. At the moment, Lee handled both the budgeting referred to
earlier and the competitive evaluation of TV commercials.
Budgeting was by far the more important of the two subjects

—usually, any position closer to the money is the more important one.

But the job might soon be split into the two different functions, and Lee was pretty sure that Bo was angling for the budgeting part, with Lee shunted aside into the job of competitive evaluation. This was largely a research job, which Lee thought had very little future and could be eliminated at the first suspicion of hard times.

The V.P. of production had the authority to make the switch, and Lee had told him that he didn't want the research job. Lee was also pretty certain that Bo had let the V.P. know that he wanted the budgeting job. This was the game. What should Lee do?

Lee decided he had several options:

- He could do nothing, in other words, continue to do his job and nothing but his job.

- He could match Bo's hangout strategy by spending more time hobnobbing with the V.P. of production.

- He could try to end the game by finding an expert at the competitive analysis of commercials, *with no financial background,* to push for that spot should it open up.

Lee applied the Basic Decision-making Principle of Game Theory to each of his choices:

"If I do nothing, what I don't want but am afraid I might get is that Bo will continue to hang out with my boss. I'm likely to lose then. I say 'likely' because guys who constantly politic sometimes self-destruct; you know, they say something to offend the guy they're trying to butter up. I don't think there's much chance of this with Bo—he's pretty smooth—but it's always possible.

"If I try to match Bo at politics, the problem is that I can't. I'm simply not that good at it. So what I don't want but am afraid

I might get is that I'll self-destruct. If I don't, great—I beat Bo. But if I do screw up, I'm in big trouble.''

Which is worse, doing nothing and letting Bo run away with it, or doing something and screwing up?

"I don't know. They're both equally bad. I mean, socializing is something you can either do well or you can't.

"If I try my third choice, finding someone else for the research job, what I don't want but am afraid I might get is that my boss, the V.P. of production, will be annoyed that I was meddling in his job. But then I'll know how I really stand with him. I guess this is best.''

And this is exactly what he did. He hunted all over for a plausible expert on commercials. He finally found one, a twenty-three-year-old black woman, a straight-A student fresh out of graduate school. The agency's affirmative action officer had just berated all the V.P.s for not achieving their affirmative action goals. When the new spot opened up she got it, at a much lower salary than Lee would have gotten. This was Lee's ostensible selling point. Without the research job opening, there was no way the V.P. could get rid of Lee. Bo gave up and stopped hanging out with the V.P. He had been muscled out of the picture.

The key to this solution from Lee's standpoint was realizing the asymmetry of the situation. He had an extra option that Bo didn't have—namely, coming up with an outside candidate. Bo couldn't do this because Lee was generally recognized as doing an extremely good job. Therefore, he couldn't simply be fired. This gave Lee the chance to end the rivalry by eliminating the incentive for it.

There are several lessons from Game Theory in situations such as this:

- **Examine your option of hanging out very carefully. Can you really match the social charm of your rival? If so, great. But if not, you might simply seal your fate by trying to match him with what will be viewed as a pathetic version of his strategy.**

- Consider very carefully the possibility that your rival might self-destruct. Those who use the hang-out strategy often do.

- See if there are special advantages that you might have over your rival, strategies which you have that he doesn't. A common one is to bring in some-one against him, one who meets a need that your rival can't.

33

Muscling the Extremely Brazen

A LOT OF PEOPLE got where they are by being brazen. They never take no for an answer. They simply barge ahead, keep talking, and make the sale. With this attitude, they go from strength to strength. In a way, their courage is admirable. You've really got to hand it to them, and if you have any business dealings with them, you probably will if you're not careful.

Have you taken a good look at how they operate? They bully. It's as simple as that. They figure out what it is about somebody that allows that person to be intimidated, and they use it. They often have trouble intimidating those who know what they're doing, so the extremely brazen often go after the inexperienced, the ones who don't yet know which end is up. Game Theory can be very helpful to the inexperienced when they confront the extremely brazen.

This was the case with Pamela. She is an assistant vice presi-dent of sales at a major San Francisco consumer products company. She works on in-house sales promotions. The company holds extravaganza in-house shows for its sales force and contracts with independent producers to set them up. One independent producer had had a bad track record of coming in over budget, and Pamela's company had always paid the difference. Why did her company keep dealing with the producer? There were two reasons:

- He did good work.

- For reasons that nobody Pamela talked to fully understood, he had the confidence of key officers of the company.

However, as a result of his bad track record on billing, the legal department had drawn up a very tight contract for $150,000, and not one penny more.

At the sales promotion show, Pamela noticed the producer spent a lot of time hobnobbing with senior executives of the company. They joked around like old friends. At one point, the thought crossed Pamela's mind that the producer had deliberately wandered around with the CEO just so she and a few others there would see them together. But she quickly dismissed the thought from her mind as silly. The producer was known to be gay, and there had been hints that the CEO, although married, was gay as well. The occasional raised eyebrow from persons other than Pamela made her believe that she wasn't the only one who suspected an affair might be taking place. This was fine as far as she was concerned. Who either of these gentlemen slept with was none of her business, she felt, providing they didn't want to sleep with her, and neither of them did.

In any case, the show was a big hit, and the senior officers of the company went around afterward talking about how great it had been. The producer immediately got another job from the company to do the show for the next line.

Then the bill arrived. The producer wanted an extra $25,000 for special equipment and additional labor expenses that had not been originally anticipated. The bill went directly to Pamela's desk, since she was in charge of approving or rejecting such matters. Her problem was what to do now.

She was new in her job, and this show was the first she had worked on. She went to her boss for guidance, but he didn't want to discuss it. "It's your responsibility," he told her. There was no way she could pass the buck. She had to deal with it. She used Game Theory to assess her own and the producer's relative vulnerability.

Pamela decided she had three options:

- She could stonewall the producer and pay nothing more.

- She could pay him the full $25,000.

- She could negotiate with him, try to feel out exactly what his contact was with top management, and if necessary, pay no more than half his extra bill.

Her temptation, on receiving the bill and getting the brushoff from her own boss, was to start negotiations with the producer, with the possible aim of settling for half. However, before doing so, she applied Game Theory to analyze her choices:

"If I stonewall, what I don't want but am afraid I might get is that the producer will sue the company. This would be bad, because it would be very awkward to use him again in the future, and top management, especially the CEO, seems to like him. I'll look as if I've mishandled the situation. Also, if there is some kind of funny business going on between the producer and the CEO, they won't say anything now, but they'll settle my hash later on some other pretext. Altogether, I'm vulnerable with this choice.

"If I pay the full $25,000, what I don't want but am afraid I might get is that top management will call me in and challenge me on it. Then what am I going to say, 'I thought the producer was the CEO's homosexual lover, so I thought I'd help them feather their love nest'? I don't think that would go over too well. And I can't defend the payment based on the contract, so what could I say? Altogether, I'd be extremely vulnerable. So this is a worse choice than the other one.

"If I negotiate, with the possibility of settling for half, what I don't want but am afraid I might get is everything in the previous choice. What difference does it make if I pay half or all if I'm not supposed to pay any? I thought I could negotiate, but I realize now that if I do, it implies some basis for negotiation, and there isn't any."

Pamela then evaluated her best strategy, stonewalling, to see what the producer didn't want but was afraid he might get. She made a list of the options open to the producer if she stonewalled:

• The producer could sue her company.

• The producer could complain to his friend, the CEO, if he was his friend.

Pamela then evaluated each of the producer's options, if she stonewalled:

"If he sues, the company will close ranks against him. They won't be happy about it, but that's what they'll do, and he won't get any more work. So he's locked out of that choice.

"If he complains to his presumed friend, the CEO, what can the CEO do? He can order me to pay the bill, but then it's his responsibility, not mine. Or he can do nothing now and get back at me later for interfering in his affairs. It's fifty-fifty whether he would do this, but this is better than the bad part of my other choices, and at least I'd know where I stand. I think, all things considered, that I can muscle the producer into dropping his request for more money, and then it's fifty-fifty whether there will be repercussions due to 'extraneous factors.' "

She stonewalled. The producer dropped his request for more money, and she still doesn't know if there is any hanky-panky between the CEO and the producer, and she doesn't care, because so far, it hasn't affected her job at all.

There are several lessons to be learned from Game Theory

in situations in which somebody tries to muscle you by appearing to be pals with influential persons at your company:

- **Don't let anyone intimidate you. Before doing *anything*, use Game Theory just as you would in any other situation.**

- **Look at each of your choices to see where you are vulnerable. In other words, when looking at what you don't want but are afraid you might get, pay particular attention to what the other guy can do to you.**

- **After you determine your best strategy, give it a second look from the standpoint of what your rival can do to you. Make a list of his responses to see if you really can lock him in where you want him. If your strategy looks okay, go ahead with it.**

34

How to Be a Good Colonial Administrator of a Subject Company

WE ALL KNOW THAT during the heyday of the British Empire the British colonial administrators played cricket and polo, dressed with understated good taste, took tea in the afternoon, and always wore dinner jackets at dinner. But this elegant style was not the basis of their astonishing colonial success. They did not cow the natives of half the globe by being potential covers for

Gentlemen's Quarterly. Their leisured elegance was a by-product of a single, and very simple, colonial policy: Wherever they could, they tried to get local crooks to do the dirty work for them.

In India, they made deals with as many of the feudal lords, the maharajas, as they could. The maharajas used traditional methods, whatever they may have been and however offensive they might seem to us and to the British people now. Occasionally, these traditional methods even seemed offensive to the British at the time, as when some British officers were incarcerated in "The Black Hole of Calcutta" by some mutinous local bigwigs.

Although, in hindsight, we might think the British imperial policy to be brilliant, or at least very clever, it was, in fact, the only policy that could have worked. The upper classes of Victorian Britain did not trust the lower classes and were not about to give millions of them sufficient education to run the day-to-day affairs of an empire. They made that kind of mistake in the thirteen colonies, the leaders of which started writing such heresies as "all men are created equal." Instead, they made deals with the local power structures wherever they could, providing the British got their piece of the action. And that's how they ran the larger part of the globe. In short, this was the British imperial administrative policy:

- Keep the British imperial civil service small, upper-class, and very much of an elite.

- Make maximum use of local bigwigs.

The British Empire lasted hundreds of years with these policies. And, with many reforms and much social justice, a few bits and pieces of it remain more or less happily ensconced in it to this day.

Earlier in this century, another empire tried a different administrative policy, but got away with it for only about ten

years. That's how long Hitler's Third Reich lasted. Its administrative policy was the exact opposite of the British one:

- Maximize the presence of Nazi "civil servants," e.g., the
  Gestapo and armed personnel. In some areas, such as
  Eastern Europe, colonize with Germans.

- Destroy local power structures if possible. Make minimum use of them if destruction isn't feasible. If they
  must be tolerated, keep them under the closest possible
  surveillance and make sure they do things the Nazi way.

We needn't detain ourselves with the horrible consequences of these policies. The interesting thing is that the lessons of the very successful British colonial civil service are so
often ignored, despite its astonishing success, and at least the
nonviolent aspects of the Third Reich are so often followed, despite that regime's obvious failure.

What I am getting to, of course, is the most prominent single
feature of American business at this time—*takeovers.* There are
two types:

- "Friendly" takeovers: Top management of the gob-
  bled-up company endorses the deal.

- "Unfriendly" takeovers: Top management of the prey
  fights back, even when it's in the predator's mouth.

Of course, from the viewpoint of the critical number of
stockholders needed to gain control, all takeovers appear, at
least initially, to be friendly to them. Otherwise they wouldn't
sell. However, from the standpoint of the middle manager or supervisor in the taken-over company, the situation feels terrify-
ingly similar to that of a citizen of an occupied country:

- A new management "team" suddenly arrives from the
  "parent" company, and its members give the orders,
  even if they don't know what they are doing.

- The managers in the acquired company often have a group solidarity against the new overlords, like the Anglo-Saxons against the Normans.

- The jobs of whole groups of managers in the acquired company may be "liquidated," even if none of them is individually "guilty" of any bad judgment or any other kind of wrongdoing. Many of these managers may find themselves unemployable at other major companies.

- The careers of most middle managers in the acquired company may be permanently stunted, simply because they aren't from the parent company. They can settle for second-class status, or they can "emigrate" to other companies or other jobs, becoming refugees of the take-over.

This is the situation Alex found himself in. Originally from Hungary, he was literally a refugee from Hitler who had arrived in Miami by way of a displaced persons camp in 1948. After a series of jobs, Alex became the supervisor of an art shipping company, employing about fifty persons, most of whom were black and Hispanic. Alex had successfully supervised this company for the past fifteen years.

This was a family-owned business doing a specialized kind of shipping of very expensive, very delicate objects. It was a highly profitable business at the time of the death of the founder, and the heirs sold it at a good price to a huge conglomerate. They sent an administrator, Christine, to run it. She did an excellent job on the financial aspects of the business, but wisely left the supervisorial tasks where they had been for the past decade and a half, with Alex.

That is, she did until the incident. Alex caught one of his workers doing a dangerously shoddy packing job. This, in itself, was not unusual, nor was the worker's denial of his responsibility. Alex's outrage at the unwillingness of the worker to own up to the facts also wasn't unusual. Over the years, this had happened off and on. Alex would write up a disciplinary report, the worker would be given a warning, and if the incident was repeated, the worker would be out. Incidentally, if a worker admitted the error, Alex wouldn't write up anything but would mumble something about, "We all make mistakes." If the confessing worker continued to do a sloppy job, Alex would simply switch him to a less critical job. In this way, Alex was both feared and loved by the crew.

What made this particular incident unusual was the presence of the unknown quantity, Christine. The worker complained to her about Alex, saying, essentially, that he was too much of an authoritarian. Christine, who thought of herself as a liberal, took the side of the Hispanic worker. She said later that she felt that the lower-class minority, and therefore presumed unhappy, background of the man should be given some weight in the case. When asked why she didn't think the same considerations should be made for Alex's known unhappy background, Christine said that there were special difficulties for repressed groups in America, and that she was pretty sure Alex was racially prejudiced against this worker and most of the others who worked there.

In any case, when Alex went to put his report on file, Christine strongly urged him to reconsider. During a heated discussion, he told her point-blank that she didn't understand the way things worked at this company. She reminded him that she was the new administrator from corporate headquarters, and that she had the power. He tore up his report and went back to his office.

For the next two months, Alex's authority seemed to slip away from him. Quite a bit of sloppiness was found in the work, and although most of the workers admitted their mistakes, an increasing number did not. Alex, still pained from the earlier experience, did not write up any of them. After three months he retired early. Christine had a great deal of difficulty replacing Alex, and in that interim the word quickly spread among the museums, galleries, and private collectors that had used the company for many years. Business dropped off considerably. There were several layoffs, and then the business was closed and the facilities were sold off. Christine revealed the details of the incident in her exit interview.

She told me about the incident a year after it had happened. She applied Game Theory in hindsight. This is not, of course, the best way to use the theory, but it revealed an interesting fact—the obvious merit of the British imperial civil service procedures:

"If I had backed up Alex against the worker, what I wouldn't have wanted but probably would have gotten was a specific instance of injustice against this one employee. Things would have continued exactly as they had for the past fifteen years.

"If I had backed up the worker against Alex, which of course is what I did, what is it that I wouldn't have wanted but should have been afraid I might get? The answer is clear now, and was then—the disruption of a successful, in other words profitable, power structure. At the time, I wanted to disrupt the power, but I didn't ask myself what that might do to the profit. I lost my job and caused the loss of jobs for a lot of people because I looked only at what I wanted, instead of what I didn't want."

Earlier, I contrasted the British imperial administration with that of the Nazis. What Christine did followed neither the letter nor the spirit of the Nazis. Nonetheless, like the Nazi occupations, it was a meddling strategy, and the meddling led to her undoing. Of course, if she had been there a while, and really gotten to know what was going on, she might have figured out how to meddle in subtle ways and get away with it.

There are two lessons from Game Theory for the manager from corporate sent to manage a profitable unit of an acquired company:

- **Keep the British model of colonial administration in mind as a guide. In so far as possible, try to make use of the existing power structures.**

- **Before making any alterations in the existing power structure, apply the Basic Decision-making Principle of Game Theory.**

35

When You Are Muscled by Prominence

YOU'RE GOING TO HAVE a business meeting with someone. One of you is about to name the time. He might say 10:45 tomorrow morning, or 3:00 in the afternoon, and if he is known to be very busy, or has much higher social status than you do, you might not question these times. But if he is more or less a peer, he would have to give an explanation for these times, and his explanation could perhaps be misinterpreted to imply that his time is more valuable than yours. So unless he has a good reason for the unusual time, he's much more likely to simply suggest, "Lunch tomorrow."

There is absolutely nothing offensive, arrogant, or presumptuous about the suggestion of lunchtime as the meeting time. Of course, if you can't make it, then you are perfectly free to explain why not. But to avoid the appearance of arrogance, you must either agree or explain. Why? Lunchtime is a customary time for a business meeting. It overshadows other times. To use a bit of jargon from Game Theory, lunchtime is *prominent.*

Prominence is the characteristic of something that removes ambiguity.

This is why the offer of lunch removes possible unwanted connotations that the suggestion of an unusual time might create. Notice that the two parties are talking to each other. There's nothing holding them back from arranging some other time for the meeting—except the effort of doing so. But this is enough. Prominence has muscled it off the agenda.

Prominence often effectively removes subjects from the agenda of negotiation, because to bring up such topics might be to fly in the face of standard procedures, and nobody wants to open up that can of worms. Pay raises can work this way. They may be on some uniform scale, and the request for the raise must hit one of the prominent points or else it may be viewed as asking for too much, however just the request might be.

Ironically, holding the meeting over lunch keeps the focus of attention not on padding the expense account but on the business. This is one reason so many business persons scream whenever Congress starts to talk about changing the tax deductions on the "three-martini lunch." Other reasons they scream are:

- They like to pad their expense accounts.

- It is much more fun to eat at "21" than McDonald's, especially, maybe even only, if the company is picking up the tab.

- The office is driving them nuts, and they need an excuse to get out.

- At a fancy restaurant, they will be treated differently from the way they are at their offices. In other words, they'll be treated well.

Thank heaven for little prominences. Without them what would business life be? Very confusing. Something is prominent if it allows you and the person you are dealing with to coordinate your expectations. Almost anything can serve this purpose, a social custom, for example. In some Wall Street brokerage houses the men smoke cigars. They like to look macho? Some do, but if they don't smoke cigars they won't look the part. They'll stand out. And what is most prominent about these brokerage houses is that nobody looks prominent.

Sometimes the prominence can lead to unavoidable inefficiency. You are desperate to sign a contract, but you must keep it at least overnight, ostensibly to think it over. In fact, you've thought about nothing else for the past six months. But you know that the other party doesn't know this and expects you to think it over. Otherwise, you might look overeager, too hungry. Prominence has slowed things down.

There are different ways by which prominence can be achieved:

Time	Certain times are simply more noticeable than others. They even have specific names: noon, midnight. Other noticeable times are 9:00 A.M. and 5:00 P.M., the usual beginning and end of the workday.
Date	Certain dates are also prominent: July 4th, for example. Even if you're not patriotic, would you schedule a business meeting on that day? You might try, but you'd have to come up with a good reason. Rents are due on the first of the month. Many contracts begin or fall due on the first business day of the new year. Another day could be argued for, but why? That one is prominent.
Place	Within your industry, there is probably a prominent meeting place. For example, for Broadway, it is traditionally Sardi's; for Hollywood, the Polo Lounge of the Beverly Hills Hotel. Incidentally, both Broadway and Hollywood are places, but they are synonymous with industries precisely because they are prominent places for those industries.

Custom

Fighting over the check is a silly practice, especially since it usually goes on a corporate expense account anyway. But try to sit back and let the other guy pay with *his* company's money. Bad connotations could cross the payer's mind, which we will list in order of increasing seriousness: (1) You lack proper social graces. (2) You're not macho. (3) You're cheap. (4) You're broke. (5) You are not important enough to have a corporate expense account.

Price

Money may increase in units as small as a penny, but not every one of those units constitutes *a price*. In many industries prices have to obey certain forms. If they don't, they are the sign of a rank amateur, with whom one cannot negotiate in good faith. For example, in publishing, contract prices with the author of a book must go in standard jumps or they don't constitute *a price*. This can mean that certain "split the difference" compromises are impossible to achieve, because they don't land on a recognized price.

Order

Being first is always prominent, although not always desirable. The first Americans to hit the beaches at Normandy were also the first of the invading Allied Army to die there. But usually, first means winning the prize. Of course, many companies have done very well by using a strategy of following the leader. But don't try arguing at a corporate meeting in favor of coming in second.

Age	All the "senior" officers at Home Box Office are in their early to mid-thirties. At other companies the senior officers live up to their description. Age is prominent, and someone outside the key age group would have to do some fast and long talking to explain why that shouldn't be a consideration for promotion.
Beauty	Take a look at the people who work in many of the "glamour" industries—fashion, movies, popular music—and you'll see why they're called *glamour* industries. Beauty is prominent. If you're not gorgeous you can still succeed—the world isn't that bad—but it's harder.
Race, Religion, Sex	These are often unspoken criteria for advancement in certain companies. They can't, with certain exceptions, be written or spoken as valid criteria, because to do so is now, fortunately, illegal in the United States. But making something illegal makes it no less prominent.

Prominence removes ambiguity, but you might prefer the looseness. You can fight prominence, but you'll probably lose. Georgia was in this situation. Thirty and hardworking, she was recently made manager of the promotions department at a large Houston cosmetics company, which we'll call Lipstick, Inc. At the first meeting of the department she ran into trouble. A copywriter with a reputation for nastiness struck the first blow against her authority with a particularly sarcastic comment. Georgia had always thought of herself as laid-back, easygoing, and completely confident in her own ability. So the nasty copywriter's remark left her totally unfazed, in fact, slightly amused.

What surprised Georgia, however, was the reaction of all the other persons at the meeting, all of whom were her subordinates. Their heads all turned in unison to look at Georgia's reaction. When she said absolutely nothing to the nasty copywriter, they seemed a bit puzzled. It turned out that the custom at Lipstick is to be tough with smart alecks. Not taking any crap from them is prominent. For some reason, firing the smart alecks is not prominent. Why this should be so remains a puzzle to everyone. But managers who do not "stand up for themselves," as the people there say, are viewed as pushovers, undeserving of respect. Georgia, who was new to the company, found all this out after the meeting, when she had lunch with the V.P. of advertising. Georgia told him that she felt like a fool making an issue out of some idiot's childish remark. "But that's the kind of fool who succeeds here," he warned her.

She decided she had several options:

- She could publicly reprimand the nasty copywriter.

- She could privately reprimand her.

- She could send a memo to everyone in her department, with a carbon copy to the V.P. of advertising, saying she wouldn't tolerate unconstructive and malicious comments.

Georgia analyzed her options using the Basic Decision-making Principle of Game Theory:

"If I privately reprimand her, what I don't want but am afraid I might get is that she'll listen quietly and then do it again at the next meeting. This would be the worst, because in the eyes of the others in the department, I would have failed to even try to establish myself.

"If I publicly reprimand her, what I don't want but am afraid I might get is a public scene. I hate public scenes. This would be awful.

"If I send the memo to everyone, what I don't want but am afraid I might get is to be accused of overreacting. But that's okay, because what they don't like here are milquetoasts; crazies are okay. This is my best strategy."

She sent the memo. It got a few sneering remarks from the nasty copywriter, but nods of approval from the others, with comments such as, "She's *really* tough." It worked: Georgia established her authority by getting herself on the prominent path.

There are two major lessons from Game Theory in this example:

- **Find out what is prominent at your company.**

- **Unless you have a lot of energy for a fight, go with whatever is prominent.**

36

How to Outmaneuver an Office Shark, or How to Take the High-*handed* Road

NO ONE CAN *learn* to be a shark. Either you're born one or you aren't. In the battle between the real shark and the one in the rented shark suit, guess which one is most likely to win? If you can't out-shark an office shark, you might nonetheless be able to outmaneuver him. Game Theory can give you some pointers.

Why was the shark in *Jaws* so terrifying? Because it was big? Sure, but there was another reason. That shark never gave up. It kept swimming around and gobbling up innocent victims even beyond a gluttonously healthy appetite. After a while the movie made the point—the shark wasn't in it for the calories, it was in it for the pure pleasure of being a shark. Sharks have more fun.

They like their work and therefore are committed to it. They will continue to act in the most sharkish manner no matter whether they are after minnows, whales, or rowboats. The bait makes no difference to them.

Office sharks are the species we should be especially concerned with. We have noted that sharks are committed to their work, every aspect of it, especially the more sanguinary parts. This brings up an extremely interesting point from Game Theory, the concept of commitment. How do you make your promises or threats believable? In other words, how does the person you are trying to muscle with a threat come to believe you'll carry it out?

How about the shark in your office? How do you deter him or her from doing something you don't like? How do you make effective threats? Threaten a shark? Forget it. While you're waving your finger he'll take off your arm. And your puny little commitments will mean nothing to a shark. Your commitments will be to a specific issue. His or her commitment is to being a shark, all the time, everywhere. Threatening will get you eaten right away, and long-term commitment to one issue will simply get you eaten on some other issue. Forget about commitment when dealing with a shark in office politics, it's a phony issue.

Sharks act on instinct alone and do not trust a reasoned approach. This is in fact the definition of an office shark:

a person who acts in a totally ruthless manner, and totally on the basis of intuition.

A senior vice president at a major movie company once told me: "You can't learn business. Business is simply common sense with jargon." There spoke a true shark. This is precisely why you cannot learn to be a shark. Either you've got it or you haven't.

Sharks don't understand their actions, they simply do them. They may not even understand their victims. Why should they?

They don't study them, they eat them. If they studied them, they might lose their appetites.

If you are confronted with a shark in the office, you basically have only three strategies:[1]

- You can try to kill it—in other words, destroy its career at your company.

- You can move on to safer waters—in other words, leave the company.

- You can temporarily outmaneuver it.

How to kill office sharks is an extensive topic far beyond the scope of this book. Moving to safer waters is always an option, providing they really are safer. How do you know there won't be sharks at the new job?

This leaves only the strategy of temporarily outmaneuvering the shark. *Maneuvering* is a subject that has received some attention in Game Theory.

Lucy had a problem with a shark in her company, a large home furnishings textile company. Lucy was head of sales incentives. Her department was supposed to come up with plans to encourage the sales force to pull some extra business. Although originally conceived as gravy, the additional sales had become much more the basis for sales campaigns than anyone had previously anticipated. In fact, what would happen is that sales, basically the turf of the marketing department, would be lousy during the first three quarters, and then the business would be virtually pulled out of the fire with a massive selling effort during the fourth quarter. Lucy's department had to come up with the gimmicks to rescue the sales efforts. Knute Rockne speeches weren't working anymore. She had to think of tangible rewards.

The sales force actually worked in the marketing department, which was also in charge of product line mix, delivery

---

[1] There is, arguably, a fourth strategy—making some kind of deal with the shark. Please see Chapter 30, and also Part VI.

dates, and pricing. Who was the shark? The head of marketing. He had eaten his way to his present position, and was now planning to gobble up the incentives department and digest it as part of marketing. This would put Lucy out of a job.

She and the shark had come up with rival plans to rescue the fourth-quarter sales. The shark's plan wasn't exactly inspiring. Its goal wasn't to sell, but to make Lucy look bad. Lucy's plan was better but the shark wasn't happy with it, because he hadn't thought of it. He wanted full credit for the fourth-quarter turnaround as his way to dump Lucy. The president hadn't seen either plan, but he would at a forthcoming meeting. The usual procedure was for incentives and marketing to agree on a plan before presenting it to the president. They usually got their way, because he relied on their judgment. If they didn't agree they would both look bad, and there was no telling what might happen. Lucy wanted the shark to agree to her plan, but the shark wanted Lucy to agree to his.

Lucy had one advantage. The shark had a reputation for being a shark. Accusing a shark in public of being a shark does not have quite the same power as holding up a mirror to the face of a vampire, but it nevertheless is a card that can be played. Both Lucy and the shark knew this, and knew that the shark was trying to soft-pedal his reputation for viciousness. He wasn't trying to stop being vicious, he just didn't want people to talk about it.

Lucy flooded the shark with a stream of memos pointing out the advantages of her proposal and the severe disadvantages of his. The volume of memos was really quite staggering, and each called for a detailed reply. Of course, sharks do not want to get bogged down in detailed, reasoned replies. The shark tried to schedule a face-to-face meeting to answer her charges, but Lucy always managed to come up with a very good excuse. And each excuse was also an opportunity for another lengthy memo. The shark practically drowned from too many memos clogging his gills.

Lucy was using a classic maneuvering strategy, as expressed

in Corollary Eight to the Basic Decision-making Principle of Game Theory:

> **In an unrepeated situation, in which you and some-one else can both gain, you can sometimes get your own way in the outcome by being able to send mes-sages but not receive them.**

Lucy was, of course, perfectly capable of receiving written messages, but the shark wasn't capable of writing them. Without face-to-face conversation, he had no way to get his message across. Lucy's last memo, which accompanied her proposal at the meeting, was a classic: "I believe incentives and marketing are in agreement on the incentives proposal for the fourth quarter. Please see the attached copies of memos. None of the points in them has been raised as an obstacle by marketing, despite over a month in which to do so."

At the meeting with the president, the shark simply nodded his head and smiled, showing a lot of teeth.

There are several lessons from Game Theory in this chapter:

- **When dealing with a shark, you are up against someone who does not obey the usual rules of rationality.**

- **Don't waste your time threatening a shark. Either do the hard stuff or don't.**

- **Don't try to become a shark. Either you've got it or you don't.**

- **Don't worry about committing yourself when dealing with a shark. The issue is irrelevant. The shark is permanently committed to being a shark, you are not.**

- **You may be able to outmaneuver a shark. Often this will simply involve the ploy of being able to send messages but not receive them. You may be**

able to exploit the intellectual limitations of the shark.

37

When You Are Muscled by an Office Fanatic

THIS BOOK IS ABOUT office politics, but what happens when community, national, or international politics enters the office? Suppose there's a hot national issue that some people at the office are squaring off over, and you have an opinion on it, too. Should you chime in with your two cents' worth? You could, but these things sometimes get pretty heated, and if nothing is to be gained, perhaps something will be lost. The Basic Decision-making Principle of Game Theory would obviously tell you to keep your mouth shut.

Salespeople are constantly in this position. They're near closing a deal when the customer starts sounding off on some political or social topic. Let's say the salesman finds the customer's remarks abhorrent. Does he run the risk of throwing the sale in the garbage can by bravely confronting the utterly wrong-headed and maybe even bigoted customer? It could happen. But usually the salesman takes the position that the customer is entitled to his opinion, just as the salesman is entitled to the customer's money.

Salespeople have come up with lots of tricks to implement this strategy. They can agree with the opinionated customer, ask him to go on about it, ask for the names of books on the subject (risky, because the loudmouth usually hasn't read any), ask to be put on the appropriate mailing list. All the while they are steering the customer's hand closer and closer to the dotted line. One salesman told me that the customer sometimes wants an argument. And the salesman gives him one, a losing one, of course. The customer is sold the product, and the salesman says he is sold on voting for the customer's party at the next election. Another salesman told me that after an incident such as this he sometimes makes a small donation from the commission he receives to the opponents of the wrongheaded customer.

The salesman has the advantage of making the sale and then getting the hell out of there. Whenever you are forced to listen to an opinionated blowhard at the office, however, you may well have a sinking fear that this won't be the last time. He'll be at it again tomorrow and the next day. Most people in offices avoid like the plague anything inflammatory. And the only topic at the office more inflammatory than politics is religion. Both subjects tend to get people worked up, so both are avoided as topics of conversation at most companies. This puts you in the driver's seat. By dodging political issues, you are expressing the norm; the fanatic is exposing himself to fire. If the fanatic is a peer, you can easily tell him to keep his opinions to himself. But what do you do when your boss starts pushing his political views on you?

Several middle managers from the same large manufacturing company told me about feeling a subtle pressure to contribute to the corporate political action committee. They thought it expedient to kick in the minimal amount, and they did, even though they didn't know which candidates would later get the money. However, that was the end of it; they weren't pressured further on political issues. This is interesting. Managers at this company looked, dressed, and talked the same, but they didn't think or presumably vote the same. They all knew it, and they avoided talking about politics.

This problem is particularly prevalent in the media. A writer for a syndicated daily TV show dealing principally with feature stories was suddenly pressured by his boss, the head writer, to insert a political angle into the stories. The angle didn't fit; it just cluttered the stories. The writer told this to the boss, who insisted. The writer simply refused to insert it, arguing that he didn't know enough about the political angle to do it justice. The boss then went on at great length, arguing his side of this political issue, trying to draw out the writer and engage him in a political discussion. But the writer simply refused to take the bait. He told me: "I wouldn't discuss politics. I said I didn't have to account to anyone for my political beliefs, which is why we have a secret ballot in this country. I realized that if I took the position of no baloney and all business, I was in the stronger position."

His strategy was quite clever from a Game Theory standpoint. By claiming ignorance, he forced the fanatic to be even more outspoken. This was temporarily unpleasant, but it clearly established the situation for what it was—a blatant attempt by the boss to muscle the writer along political lines. This helped to protect the writer against possible subsequent charges of connivance. The writer explained his thinking:

"If I had ultimately knuckled under and inserted the political angle, what I didn't want but was sure I'd get is flak from the producer. He's on the ball and would have caught the propaganda angle. Then he'd either have cut it out or asked me what gives. Even though I'd have passed the buck to the head writer, the producer might have thought I showed bad judgment. This is serious, because the producer determines contract renewals.

"By refusing to insert the political angle, I took a lot of immediate heat from the head writer. This was bad, but a lot better than losing the confidence of the producer. I didn't think they could fire me for refusing to make my stories political. They'd have to build up a case on some other matters, and that would take time. But the ideologue didn't have much time because I wasn't the only one he was haranguing. He was wasting a lot of people's time with his political claptrap, alienating a lot of people. Within two months the producers transferred him to another project where his job was to do absolutely nothing. The producer told me he didn't want to fire him or he'd be accused of firing someone for political reasons."

This seems quite often to be the case. The bullying office fanatic draws unfavorable attention to himself and self-destructs.

The process is almost inevitable, because the basic ideology of
the office is not whatever the fanatic is peddling but is instead
the position probably taken by the fanatic's boss—"all business
and no baloney." The best strategy is usually to try to avoid confrontation, to claim ignorance of the issues as your basis for refusing the political intrusion, and to point out your constitutional right to the privacy of your opinions. Then sit back and let
the fanatic hang himself.

There are several lessons from Game Theory in this chapter:

- **There is rarely anything to be gained by chiming in
  on office discussions of politics, but there is sometimes something to be lost if the discussions get
  too heated.**

- **You can almost never be fired for refusing to discuss your political views.**

- **You can smoke out the fanatic by claiming ignorance of the political issue. If he bends your ear
  about it, he clearly labels himself as the agitator,
  and you can't be accused of subtly conniving with
  him.**

- **Those who insist on bending your ear on their political cause are bound to alienate a lot of people
  and could be accused of not getting the job done,
  since they aren't taking the position of all business
  and no baloney.**

- **The best strategy to use against a boss whose politics interferes with your work is to avoid confrontation as best you can. You can claim ignorance
  of the issues, refuse to participate in his politics
  based on your constitutional right to the privacy
  of your own views, and sit quietly as he self-
  destructs.**

Part 5
Whispering

38

Loose Talk Sinks Careers, Especially Yours

IN BRITAIN DURING World War II there were signs plastered all over the place: *Loose talk sinks ships.* The same rule is probably fairly well established for your company. This is either because corporate rivalry is totally cutthroat or because top management would like to give that illusion to the lower ranks. Whatever the reason, giving away company secrets is usually considered very bad form.

Many of my MBA graduate students ran into this problem. They would write term papers about their companies, major corporations headquartered in New York City, and this often made senior management very nervous. Top officers often insisted that they have the opportunity to review the papers before they were handed in. Of course, I never knew if the senior officer was concerned about company secrets or worried that the contents of the paper would reflect badly on him. Often the senior censor objected to the inclusion of data that had already been published. My students would point this out, but the senior censor had a reply ready: "Let the competitors find it out themselves, why organize it for them?"

The senior censor had a point, though not a very good one. If the competitors were on the ball they'd already have read the published information, and if they weren't on top of things they probably wouldn't put much stock in a student paper anyway. What if they didn't know it was a student paper? With these papers, you always knew, so almost nothing was at stake except the attitude of the employees at the senior censor's company. He was trying to maintain a loose-talk-sinks-ships attitude all the time.

Would it make sense to take the same attitude about your own personal career? How much free information should you give away about yourself? The answer is simple: none. None? What about some common injunctions such as "honesty is the best policy," and "always tell the truth, then you don't have to remember your lies"?

These are common injunctions, but they aren't always valid. In fact, they can be positively harmful to you if followed. For example, you've just come from a business meeting. "How did it go?" someone asks. You're tired, and you don't feel like explaining, so you blurt out: "Lousy!" *The wrong answer!* Why? If the asker is a disinterested party, you never know how the information may be used against you later. Whom will this person tell that your meeting was lousy? Do you know? Do you care? Maybe not now, but you might someday, when you discover you have given yourself a bad reputation. And all because you told something that wasn't entirely true to someone who didn't need to know.

If the asker is an interested party, what is his interest? Is it the same as yours? If so, you'll probably tell him the details anyway. Why prejudice his judgment before he hears the facts? Let him hear them. Then he can tell you the meeting went lousy or well, or give you some new insight on it.

If you're not convinced of this, apply the Basic Decision-making Principle of Game Theory:

If you tell a disinterested party the truth, what is it that you don't want but are afraid you might get? The answer is obvious—he might somehow use this information against you.

If you tell the disinterested party a lie, what is it that you don't want but are afraid you might get? Again the answer is obvious. He might later catch you out in the lie. And although this may mean nothing at the moment, your credibility on some other issue may be diminished.

If you don't tell the disinterested party anything, what is it that you don't want but are afraid you might get? Again the answer is obvious. He might think you're a bit of a bore, but that's it. You might not be invited to his dinner parties. Did you want to go? If so, run the risk of being a fool or a liar.

We have just deduced the Ninth Corollary to the Basic Decision-making Principle of Game Theory:

Never give out unnecessary information about how well you are doing, even if you are doing well.

Getting back to the dinner parties you might not get invited to: You don't have to be a bore; there's a way out. You need a cover story for all contingencies. Here it is: "Great!"

You need nothing more, nothing less. If the meeting went poorly, your tone will give you away. Let it. Let the listener try to divine the truth—that's his problem. He'll try anyway, no matter what you say, if he's interested in doing so, but he'll have to do it without your help. And if he figures the meeting went badly, he'll also figure you were speaking ironically, but he won't know for sure. That's good: Your business remains your business. Most important, no tangled web. You never have to remember what you told disinterested parties because you have politely told them nothing.

We have just learned several lessons from Game Theory:

• The concept of *loose tongues sink ships,* used and misused by many corporations concerning their businesses, can be applied to your own career. You can ask, "Why does this person need to know about my career problems?" If the person doesn't, ask yourself why you need to tell him.

• An application of the Basic Decision-making Principle of Game Theory reveals that your best strategy concerning giving out unnecessary information is that you shouldn't give out any.

- To avoid giving away any unnecessary information, you need a permanent cover story. One was
  proposed: *Great!*

39

When You Know Too Much but Are Afraid It Isn't Enough

COUNTLESS MOVIES HAVE REVOLVED around a single plot structure:
An innocent bystander finds out about something he didn't want
to know and previously had no idea existed. He usually tries to
dodge the responsibility to do good inherent in the knowledge,
but inevitably gets roped into action by circumstances beyond
his control.

This is what happened to Erika, twenty-five. She was new to
the industry, so her company, a major manufacturer of a wide
variety of largely exported machine tools, sent her to a trade association meeting. A rival firm was holding its biggest sales con-
vention in the same city at the same time. Erika foiled their security. Nobody was paying much attention when she walked
through the door wearing her trade association badge.

Following the afternoon session, she was at the buffet table
munching on raw broccoli when she overheard a conversation
between a senior vice president and a major Washington lobbyist for the rival firm. They were discussing an upcoming change
in the tax laws they were about to start pushing. The change
would favor them but be damaging to the rest of the industry, especially to Erika's company. The lobbyist mentioned the names

of key congressional aides he had been buttering up. There was an ambiguous hint of a bribe.

Erika immediately got on the phone to her company's director of public relations and told him what she had sleuthed out. She thought that would be the end of it, but it wasn't. When she got back to her hotel room, a message was waiting for her: "Return tomorrow morning to Chicago to discuss with the V.P., Legal, information gained from rival penetration."

"Rival penetration?" Erika thought she had walked into a bad joke from a James Bond movie. But she had been summoned to see a big shot, so she had to go.

She began to feel very nervous and somewhat foolish. Had she overheard the two gentlemen correctly? Was she absolutely sure they were who she had said they were? She suddenly regretted her initial phone call. She was in sales, she told me she thought to herself, so what did she know about legal mumbo jumbo? She was about to talk to a bigwig whom she had never met, about a legal issue she knew virtually nothing about, concerning a competitor about which she knew very little. Furthermore, this was her first contact with top management, and in an area she had given some thought to entering—corporate lobbying in Washington. As a result of playing cat and mouse —at her own initiative—she stood a good chance of blowing any possible credibility in that area. In fact, this was one of her major worries—would the V.P. give any credence to what she said?

She decided she had several options:

- She could talk to him to see what he wanted to know and then tell him that part of what she had heard. In other words, she could feel him out.

- She could sketch a broad outline of what she had heard and then see if he wanted more details.

- She could simply tell him everything in as much detail as possible.

Erika evaluated each of her options using the Basic Decision-making Principle of Game Theory:

"If I feel him out and wait to see what he wants to know, what I don't want but am afraid I might get is that he'll think I'm acting like a little tease trying to get something out of him in exchange for the information. I don't think that'll do my career at this company any good at all. So this option is out.

"If I just present the broad outline, what I don't want but am afraid I might get is that he won't pursue it with me, but will act on the basis of only a portion of the story. He might ignore it, and then somehow I might get blamed later if that turned out to be a mistake. How could *I* be blamed? He might say I held back key details. So this is no good either.

"If I just tell him everything, what I don't want but am afraid I might get is that I'll be nervous and distort the story, or inadvertently leave out parts. Then he might think that I'm a dope, and there goes any chance of working in his area. But at least this doesn't have the problems of the other options."

Telling all was Erika's best strategy. But she still had to deal with the problem of making sure she did tell all. She did this by writing a long memo to him, in as much detail as she possibly could, of everything she had heard. This would at least give the appearance that she knew what she was doing. She said she felt "sort of like John Dean writing down his recollections of what happened in the Oval Office."

The memo turned out to be a very good idea. The V.P. was quite impressed with her, and several months later offered her a job in the Washington lobby office.

This chapter contains several lessons from Game Theory:

- **A standard corporate game is that of unnecessary intercorporate intrigue. Don't laugh at it in the presence of the boss. He's pretending to take it seriously.**

- **If you happen upon information about a rival firm, think twice before letting anyone in your firm**

know about it. If you do let your boss know, he
will immediately relay the information upward,
out of fear of being accused of negligence if he
doesn't. Then you will instantly get caught up in
the intrigue game.

- If you have to give a report on what you know to a
big shot in your company, evaluate your options
carefully. You may well want to not only tell all,
but put it in writing as well.

40

When You Have Useful Information but Can't Use It Without Revealing That You Have It

INSIDER INFORMATION IS OFTEN billed as the little guy's shot at the
big score. Typists in legal offices that specialize in corporate
mergers have turned it into tens of thousands of dollars. Many
executives hang out with their colleagues during the happy
hour, hoping for some information that will really make them
happy. Usually they get a hangover instead, because the information they get, however damaging it may be to someone else's social reputation, is usually of no benefit to one's professional advancement.

The Basic Decision-making Principle of Game Theory can
be used as a test for the worth to you of any piece of gossip: If

you didn't have this information, what is it that you don't want
but are afraid you might get? If the answer is that you figure
you'd end up the same with or without the information, you
know that the gossip isn't worth the price of the drink you may
have bought somebody to get it. This is in fact the traditional
definition of worthless gossip: *Worthless gossip is gossip that
isn't worth the price of a drink.*

Sometimes you get information that is worth something to
you, or at least could be, if you could use it. However, if you use
it, you may reveal that you have it, and you're not supposed to.

Where did you get the information? Inevitably it came from
someone who said, "Don't tell anyone I told you this." This sentence tags the information as a secret. Without that sentence,
expressed or implied, the information is not a secret. The information may be absolutely public, except for a public acknowl-
edgment that it is public. In other words, everyone may know,
but, if cornered, everyone would publicly deny knowing anything about it. Information of this kind, public without being acknowledged as public, has an interesting strategic property. In
Game Theory, it would be treated as perfect information. Chess
is an example of a game of perfect information. Each player
knows exactly what the other one has done in the game up to
that point. And therefore, according to a mathematical proof in
Game Theory, the outcome of the game is clear and inevitable.
This inevitability would be true of chess if the complexity of the
game didn't foil the logical capacity to work it out.

But office politics, as we have seen, is usually pretty simple,
once the underlying constraints are understood. So what would
happen in a deterministic situation that is supposed to be played
out in secret if it were suddenly brought out into the open? In
chess, it would in principle make no difference; the game would
work out exactly the same. And this is true also in office politics.
Bringing a cut-and-dried, but hidden, office game out in the
open will probably not change the outcome. Why? The underlying power relationships are unlikely to change. This is why
threatening exposure of many situations, and actually exposing
them, doesn't change very much. People go on and do what they

were going to do anyway. It will, however, anger an awful lot of them. They like to play this game, but with the bathroom door locked.

This leads to the Tenth Corollary to the Basic Decision-making Principle of Game Theory:

If the outcome of a situation is foreseeable by logical inevitability, information plays no strategic role.

In other words, a lot of secrecy in office politics is not *strategic* secrecy but *insider* secrecy. With strategic secrecy, finding out what the other guy is up to is critical to the outcome. Most of the situations described in Part II on Dueling dealt with strategic secrecy. If you can find out what he is up to you are ahead. But with insider secrecy, you can often figure out what he's up to, and usually you'd rather not be told. If you are told, the information does you no good, but if the other guy finds out that you know, he may be forced publicly to acknowledge that fact, and he may well feel that his privacy has been violated.

How do you know if information is strategic or insider? The test is very simple, and is expressed in Corollary Eleven to the Basic Decision-making Principle of Game Theory:

Strategic **information always removes critical uncertainty about the outcome.** *Insider* **information never does.**

In other words, if you can figure it out without being told, then the information is insider. If you can't, the information is strategic. This brings up the Game Theory definition of worthless gossip—*gossip that neither removes critical uncertainty nor verifies you as an insider.*

There are several varieties of insider information:

- Information that you have and can put in writing providing you don't reveal your source.

- Information that you have and can tell somebody higher in the pecking order about, but had better not put in writing.

- Information that you have but that must never be spoken or written to a person higher in the pecking order, even though he knows perfectly well that you know it.

None of these three levels of insider information, each more serious than the one before, can possibly make one jot of difference to the outcome of any given office politics game. But the improper revelation of any one of them may well determine how long you will be at the office to play future games. You could be banned from the casino, not because you're a lousy player, but because you've got lousy manners. Laying your cards on the table may sometimes be a good strategy, but only if you're playing cards. If you're playing chess, people will think you're crazy.

Can't you sometimes gain by breaking out of the rules and playing by your own rules? Maybe, if you're an independent business person, an entrepreneur. Even then you will be constrained by the social expectations of others. Within the corporate structure, forget it. No one person makes the rules, not even the CEO, unless he's been running the company for a very long time.

Heinz Nordhoff, for example, definitely put his stamp on Volkswagen. He ran the place for twenty years, rebuilding a bombed-out factory into one of the largest car manufacturers in the world. In a sense, although he died in 1967, his stamp is still on the company. Most senior management learned the ropes when Nordhoff was the boss, and there are still fewer years without Nordhoff than years with him at the top.

CEOs with shorter tenures may try to remold the way things are done at a company, and may even succeed in making some minor alterations, but for major changes they'll almost certainly fail. The rules have evolved over a long period of time. Just trying to figure out what they are is hard enough.

Willette faced this problem. She had worked in the advertising department for a magazine in Montreal. She liked the company but not her job. One day, through the grapevine, she heard about a job that was about to open up in the editorial department, which, most importantly, involved reporting directly to the editor-publisher. She had wanted to go into that area for some time, so she viewed this possible job as a tremendous opportunity for her both in terms of contacts and experience.

What should she do about this information? She was not supposed to know it, nor was she certain how many other persons, if any, knew about it. After some reflection she decided she had three options:

- She could do nothing, act as if she didn't know anything about the job, and hope the editor-publisher would give it to her on his own.

- She could talk to the editor-publisher about her career at the magazine, pointing out how interested she had always been in the editorial department and how good a background she had, and say that should any openings develop in the future, she would be interested. However, she would not say that she knew about the job. He could figure it out, but she wouldn't say it.

- She could apply for the job with no beating around the bush, telling the editor-publisher in the process that she knew about it.

Willette evaluated each of her options using the Basic Decision-making Principle of Game Theory:

"If I do nothing and hope he offers me the job, what I don't want but am afraid I might get is that the editor-publisher won't even think of me for it. Not only will I not get it, I won't even be considered. That would be the worst. So this is out.

"If I don't kid around but just apply for the job, what I don't want but am afraid I might get is the editor-publisher's grilling me on how I found out about it. Then I'd either have to refuse to tell him, which would be bad, or tell him that I'm acting on the basis of an unsubstantiated rumor, which won't exactly inspire his confidence in my editorial judgment. Or I could reveal my source, which will make me look disloyal. So this strategy could ruin the whole thing.

"If I go to him and, without mentioning that I know about the opening, tell him how much I'd like a job in the editorial department, what I don't want but am afraid I might get is that he won't give me the job. But at least I'll have put myself up for it, without embarrassing him or distracting the focus of the discussion away from the main point, the new job."

Speaking to the editor-publisher without specifically mentioning that she knew about the job was Willette's best strategy, which she used. She did not get that job because the editor-publisher had already decided on someone for it, but she did get the next good job that came up in the editorial department.

Was the information that Willette got through the grapevine strategic or insider? It had elements of both. It was strategic in a very weak sense in that she knew something was up—there was a prize to be gained. However, even without this information, she could have gone to the editor-publisher and expressed her interest in a job. She didn't have to wait for an opening to do that. So the information was basically insider, and Willette handled it with discretion.

This chapter has discussed several lessons from Game Theory:

- **You can use the Basic Decision-making Principle of Game Theory to test the value of any gossip: Without this information, what is it you don't want but are afraid you might get? If the answer is about the same with or without the gossip, the gossip is worthless.**

- **There are two types of information: Strategic information always removes uncertainty; insider in-**

formation never removes critical uncertainty, but may be no less important for that fact.

• Violating an insider taboo may be quite serious. You may not be violating the rules of the game, but you may be violating the etiquette of the game room. Be careful; you might get thrown out.

• In most situations in which you acquire apparently useful information, you can use the Basic Decision-making Principle of Game Theory to decide what to do.

41

When You Are the Target of a Vicious Smear Campaign

"IT WAS SIMPLY A meeting of the theater company," said the very successful New York television writer, as he described the incident that had occurred a few weeks earlier at a professional summer theater company that performed under an Equity contract. In an otherwise quiet meeting the writer told an actor that he was wrong on a point, and the actor promptly knocked the writer's teeth out.

The writer brought criminal charges and a lawsuit, putting the actor in deep trouble, without even Equity to turn to for protection. On his own, barred by the police and his insurance company from further violence, the actor had only his voice, his facial expressions, his body movements, and his dress at his disposal. He turned all the tricks that he uses to some success in

his trade to one purpose—bad-mouthing the writer with the
other members of the company.

He had some success at it. Most of the company had witnessed the fact that the actor was clearly the aggressor who had
made an unprovoked attack on the writer. But now the writer
was put on the defensive among the members of the company
for persecuting the poor actor—the actor who couldn't get
work, whose bills were piling up, whose children needed braces
on their teeth, etc. You get the picture—the actor was making an
underdog pitch with the company at the expense of the writer.

An underdog pitch is only one of several approaches open
to the bad-mouther. Any passable textbook on social psychology
would provide a list of them and their appeal to the target audience:

- **The pitch will work best if the audience is idle.** The
  members of the audience have nothing better to do with
  their time than get emotionally involved in your dispute
  with some other person. Also, since they are idle, they
  may have low self-esteem. The bad-mouther jacks up
  their self-esteem by flattering them into thinking that he
  values their opinions.

- **The audience should consist of bystanders.** They
  should have no legal standing in the issue. This is the
  source of their appalling sense of righteousness. They
  think they're being objective. You're only too aware
  they are being self-righteous jerks.

- **The audience may have a need for a scapegoat.**
  Things may not have been going well at the company
  lately, and the audience may be looking for a sucker on
  whom to pin the rap.

- **The members of the audience may be displacing
  their aggression.** They really want to go after a producer who isn't hiring them, but the writer is closer.

- **The audience may be identifying with the aggres-**

sor. Maybe the actor really is a tough guy, and the audience has decided nervously to smile at him and line up against his enemies.

- **The members of the audience may be insecure about their own futures.** People who are confident about their futures are less likely to fall for hate talk than are those who are insecure.

- **The audience may want to identify with an underdog.** The actor has just the guy in mind for the part.

Maybe none of the items on this list describe what was going on at the theater company. Maybe the actor was just a very smooth, charming con man. But the next time you hear badmouthing at your office, look to see who's falling for it. The odds are you'll be able to check off some items on this list. An amazing number of people in offices are standing around without much to do, with lousy jobs and low self-esteem, afraid of the boss, and thus frustrated because they can't strike back at him, worried about their futures, aware that things aren't going well in their departments, and feeling that they are bystanders to most of the action that takes place. Along comes a person who claims to be an underdog because you are victimizing him. What do you do, if anything, to counter this?

Traditional, but post-dueling, etiquette demands that you ignore the slurs unless directly confronted with them. Then you have a choice of contemptuously dismissing them or explaining, depending on the social rank of the person to whom you are talking. And under no circumstances should you bad-mouth back. A good response for right now? Maybe, maybe not. Etiquette was designed basically for one purpose—to express and maintain social distance. And if you take this high road, that's probably what you'll get—social distance. You may be accused of being distant, aloof, stuck-up, snooty. You almost certainly don't want to make yourself even less sympathetic, but that's very likely what you'll get with this choice.

On the other hand, if you counterattack the bad-mouther,

what you don't want but may very well get is to make him even
more of an underdog. This option isn't so hot either.

Then what do you do? The answer is to pick one of the
items from the above list and turn it around in your favor. If the
audience is displacing their aggression on you instead of where it
rightfully belongs—the boss?—perhaps you can see a way to re-
direct it. If the audience is insecure about its own future, maybe
in some way you can be the bearer of good news for them. This
might very quickly wash away the effects of the hate campaign.
But most effective, and easiest to do, is to out-underdog your
bad-mouther.

If you out-underdog your detractor, what is it that you
don't want but are afraid you might get? Too many flowers?

Greg, twenty-seven, an assistant controller at a large East
Coast gas company, used this strategy. A rival for a possible promotion was spreading malicious rumors that Greg was bored
with his job and therefore not putting his heart into it. As a result, so the rumor went, the poor bad-mouther was working
overtime to pick up the slack left by Greg. A classic underdog
ploy. But the fact was that Greg was very efficient and finished
his work quickly, leaving him a little time to kibitz in the corridors. The bad-mouther, on the other hand, was very slow and
plodding, and had to work overtime just to get his job done. But
Greg's boss was beginning to fall for the bad-mouthing and had
started to give Greg a hard time. "He doesn't really have his
heart in the firm," the boss was repeating. The metaphor was
what gave Greg the idea for his strategy. He checked into the
hospital for observation, complaining of chest pains. Instantly,
Greg out-underdogged the bad-mouther. Everyone felt guilty for
their harsh words. The boss went around telling everyone how
likable as well as efficient poor Greg was. Six months later, after
a physical revealed Greg in top shape, he, not the bad-mouther,
got the promotion.

Of course, this was admittedly an extreme solution; we
can't all be checking ourselves into hospitals for observation.
But I have heard of other expedients that cause the audience to
think "There but for the grace of God go I":

- A broken heart due to marital or romantic problems. All the world may still love a lover.

- Problems with the children—our actor used this one.

- Admit to the charges. Greg wasn't going to get the promotion as things stood, even though the boss knew perfectly well that Greg was doing his work. If Greg had told him he was going to make every effort to give the company 100 percent, the boss would have had to forgive him for his alleged—in fact nonexistent—slackness in the past.

- Tell everyone that you've taken the pledge. Go to a couple of A.A. meetings, even if you're a teetotaler. Everyone cheers the man who is making a real effort to get control of his life. None of them will know that your life wasn't out of control to begin with.

- Give up smoking, even if you don't smoke.

- Take up smoking at the office, because of the pressure. The crusading nonsmokers will feel guilty and immediately try to win you back to their side. Let them.

- Begin psychotherapy on the company's health plan. Discreetly tell a few people. Everyone already undergoing therapy at the office will now be more sympathetic toward you. The others will realize that you're admitting you're not perfect, but trying to do something about it.

The list could go on and you can easily add to it. The point of all these devices is simply to deflect a hate campaign against you. Select the best one for you using the Basic Decision-making Principle of Game Theory. Once the vicious talk stops, so can your device.

This chapter has revealed two lessons from Game Theory:

- **Traditional etiquette and counterattacking are probably not effective counter strategies to use**

when you are the target of a vicious smear campaign.

- An effective counter strategy is to out-underdog
  the bad-mouther.

Part 6
Siding

42

When You Are Urged to Take Sides

RECALL THE EXAMPLES IN Part II on Dueling. Nearly all of them dealt with situations in which there was a limited supply of something to be handed out—promotions, bonuses, trips. The situations were all one guy against another. But what if *groups* start to band together to advance their mutual interests? You can literally see the band in the corridors of some companies. They walk together in tight clumps. Different clumps pass each other in the hallways, and the members take stock of who's in whose faction.

Have you ever worked at a company of more than two persons that did not have factions? Probably not. If anyone tells you there are no factions in his company, that's usually a giveaway that he's in the dominant faction. You can be sure there is an out faction. It may be small, it may not be discussed, it may even be clandestine—but it's there. The logic of the situation demands it.

Consider a short list of possible bases for factions:

- **The New Guys vs. The Old Ones.** Often a new CEO will bring in a new "team" with him. There are always some holdovers from the old era. The two groups may not get along.

- **A Takeover.** The buying company usually sends some new personnel to the sold company, and they often act like an army of occupation.

- **Functional Strife.** The guys in marketing may not get along very well with the guys in production.

- **Divisional Strife.** The guys in auto parts and accessories may be competing for budget money with the guys in the sausage division.

- **The Harvard MBAs vs. Everybody Else.** In some companies, the real track to the top requires an MBA from Harvard, Stanford, or Wharton. The guys with one of those pieces of paper form a faction, sometimes even several factions. If you're not from one of those schools, you're virtually locked out. A lot of guys may be locked out, resent it, and feel themselves in the same boat, forming the boat people of the office.

- **Ethnic Strife.** There may be a dominant ethnic group that forms a sort of club among itself. For example, if that group is WASP and you're, say, Jewish, or Italian, or Polish, or Armenian, or Greek, or Asian, or Hispanic, or black, you might feel excluded from the club.

- **The Boys vs. The Girls.** Some industries, such as banking, are traditional male bastions. Others, such as publishing, have a very high percentage of women. If you're the wrong sex for your industry, you might feel the game is rigged against you.

- **The Gays vs. The Straights.** Some industries are largely dominated by gay men. Other industries, such as oil, are very macho heterosexual, and a gay man might not feel part of the inner circle.

- **Regional vs. Strangers.** Some companies have traditional roots in a specific region or city, and if you're not from there, you may always feel like a stranger and be treated like one.

This list is by no means exhaustive. But don't think for one minute that your company has only one of these or other fissures. There are probably several, and you'll become more aware of them the longer you're there. They provide a basis around which factions can form. But the important point is this: The particular demographics of a group of employees—some of which I have listed—are not necessary for the formation of factions, which will form without the need for any objective basis whatsoever. That's right. Diversity of any kind is not necessary for factions to form in your company. A company that is composed entirely of WASPs from the Northeast, all the same age, all graduates of the Harvard Business School, in one line of work only, and with no functional divisions—if that were possible— would still have factions. Corollary Twelve:

The only requirement for factions to develop in a company of more than two persons is individual greed on the part of at least one of them.

The two nongreedy ones will have to join together to protect themselves against the spoiler. But he may forestall this by making a deal with one of them against the other. The proof of this is one of the major early results of Game Theory.

We are all aware that individual greed has been a motivation for participating in business. If you're not in it at least to a large extent for the money, what are you doing there? Being an extra in somebody else's conspiracy to make money? Everybody in the office is either in it for himself or making a very big mistake being there. This is true in nearly all occupations, but in some, individuals are sometimes motivated by other things, for example, the desire for a secure, quiet life. This has attracted some people to the civil service. And what do they find when they get there? Factions.

This is what happened to Julian, thirty, married, with one child. He was a deputy director in a key division of a large department of government in a major western city. Julian was suddenly confronted with a problem of factions. He was being urged to join by two rival camps. One was headed by the assistant commissioner, Tony, forty-five, married, with three kids. Above Tony was the commissioner, appointed by the mayor. Below Tony was a chief and a director of one of the functions handled by the department. The director was Julian's immediate boss. The mayor had appointed a new commissioner for the department, and he wanted to get rid of Tony by replacing him with someone who was personally loyal. But it was not that easy because Tony had been doing a very good job.

The new commissioner, however, would see to that. Julian's boss, the director, retired, and the commissioner would not permit the job to be filled, even temporarily. Next, the chief was transferred, with no loss of salary or rank, to another city department. This left the assistant commissioner, Tony, stripped of his immediate subordinates, and put him in direct contact with someone he had previously talked to only a few times, Julian.

Incidentally, what happened to Tony is not at all uncommon in the civil service. When you fall into disfavor, the higher-ups often reduce your support staff, making your job intolerable, maybe even impossible.

Julian liked Tony, but he also knew what was happening. As a consequence of the truncation of staff, he now came in direct contact with him. And the new commissioner was watching. Julian didn't know this for sure, he only knew that the commissioner had just replaced the transferred chief, and the replacement, Carl, was paying very careful attention to Julian's relationship with Tony. He had told Julian that he was most interested in the functional matters Julian dealt with, and that he wanted to work closely with him on them. He had also hinted that if Julian played along with him, he might be promoted to the vacant slot of director.

Others in the office warned Julian not to place much stock in Carl's veiled promises. He was active in the same political party to which the mayor and the commissioner belonged, and Julian was warned that he would try to put a cohort in the vacant job.

How could Carl make him a veiled offer when he didn't have the authority to do so? Almost everybody else in the division had told Julian that Carl was about to be named the new assistant commissioner and Tony was about to be transferred, to the night shift in a branch office in the most dangerous and bombed-out section of the city.

Recall that this potential banishment was due to nothing more serious than Tony's not belonging to the mayor's faction. Tough luck? Maybe, but it became Julian's problem because Tony was fighting back, and he asked for Julian's help.

To get rid of Tony, Carl, and thus the commissioner, had to find fault with him. To do that, they needed Julian's help. The reason was simple—Carl knew absolutely nothing about the division. To push out Tony, he had to rely heavily on Julian's knowledge of divisional procedures and customs. Without this information, for which he had no source other than Julian, he could not discredit Tony. In fact, if he didn't get the information, he could fall flat on his face.

Based on this fact, Tony literally offered Julian a deal: They should team up to foil Carl, because he was simply trying to get rid of them to make room for more party hacks.

So Julian was faced with offers from two rival factions. And he had good reason to doubt the wisdom of accepting either of them. His choices were:

- Throw in with Tony against Carl and the commissioner.

- Throw in with Carl and the commissioner against Tony.

- Try to stay neutral.

At first glance, there seemed to be no contest. Julian should link with the most powerful, which would be Carl and the commissioner. But maybe not. The battle could go on for a while, and there was always the chance of a new commissioner. This was precisely the pitch Tony had used.

Julian applied the Basic Decision-making Principle of Game Theory to his choices:

"If I join Tony against Carl and the commissioner, what I don't want but am afraid I might get is that eventually they'll get rid of Tony, and then I'll be working with him on the night shift in the bombed-out neighborhood. But this would slow them down.

"If I join Carl against Tony, what I don't want but am afraid I might get is that first they'll get rid of Tony, which would be easy with my help, and then they'll get rid of me. What does Carl need me for, once he gets rid of Tony? I'm sure I wouldn't get the hinted promotion. That would go to a guy from his political club. At best I'd keep my present job, and eventually they'd probably transfer me out, too. This is pretty bad. There's really nothing in this choice for me.

"If I try to stay neutral, what I don't want but am afraid I might get is that both sides will view me as working for the other one. Tony is still my boss and could make my life miserable. And Carl, who might become my new boss, would certainly have no use for me. I'd be a loner at the mercy of every faction. So neutrality is the worst."

Julian decided that his best strategy was to throw in with Tony, reluctantly I might add. However, the strategy did buy him time. Carl called a special meeting on functional matters, expecting to get his information from Julian, but he didn't give it. He and Tony sat at a separate table at the back of the room. Carl was furious and made a total fool of himself at the meeting. After several similar fiascos he was transferred to another city department. As of this writing, the job he had occupied, the chief, is still vacant. Tony is convinced the commissioner won't fill it with anyone but a party member, but is afraid to do so now because of the attention to the case. So he won't fill it at all. As a result, both Tony and Julian are putting in a lot of overtime.

This chapter contains several lessons from Game Theory:

- **Factions will form in any organization of three persons or more, providing at least one person is greedy.**

- **Your best interests may not necessarily be in joining the new dominant faction. You should apply**

the Basic Decision-making Principle of Game Theory to make this decision.

- You may decide that you will never be fully accepted in the new winning faction.

- You may be able to prevent your boss's demise,
and it may be in your interest to do so.

43

When You Are Trying to Figure Out If You Should Switch Sides

YOU ARE EXTREMELY UNLIKELY to win if you are on your own and
are up against a faction, even a faction of half-wits. They'll always have more tricks at their disposal than you will: more information, more strategies, more time, and more energy. Bar-
ring the odd fluke, due to a faction self-destructing, we can
count on Corollary Thirteen:

The middle manager loner will always fail.

Although this statement squares with common observation
and survey data, it is not presented here as an empirical truth. It
is nothing less than a logical deduction from the Theory of
Games. So, if you fantasize yourself as Gary Cooper in *High
Noon,* or Humphrey Bogart in *Casablanca,* or Clint Eastwood in
anything, you'd better change fantasies fast. There is no corpo-

rate mileage in those fantasies. You could end up as a man without a faction.

From this we can deduce Corollary Fourteen:

To get to the top, you must join a faction whether you want to or not.

There's a catch. The mere fact that you belong to a currently winning faction doesn't mean that you will get to the top. It doesn't even mean that you'll get many or even any of the usual perks of lining up with today's winners. You may be in the winning faction, but your allies could be playing you for a sucker. Being on the winning side just means you're in the running for the perks. But if you're on the losing side, you don't even stand a chance of getting big raises, one of the best offices, an efficient secretary, or a lavish expense account with ample travel allowances.

Notice, I did not include interesting work. Even those who are part of the defeated factions often get interesting work. In fact, many persons view interesting work with the same attitude as that expressed by the ancient Chinese curse: May you live in interesting times. Interesting work is often a code term for work with too much chance for error. That kind of work usually goes to those in the out faction or to junior members of the in one.

With or without interesting work, the list sounds pretty good, doesn't it? Well, if you actually get all that stuff, it's not bad by most standards, but as I said earlier there's a catch: time. In the course of time, factions change places, and today's winning faction can become tomorrow's losing one. This doesn't necessarily mean that you will lose any of the items on the list that you currently have, but you'll probably see at least some of them slip away—your office may be shifted to a windowless room in the basement, your secretary may be promoted to someone else, and your expense account may be more rigorously scrutinized. And being on the losing side almost certainly means that you cannot do the one thing you started out in the company to do—get to the top.

Since you may be prevented from advancing by the currently powerful faction, but you hold a cushy job, probably not involving interesting work, which you got from the previous faction, you could fall into the most defaming category that exists in companies—deadwood. Look around your office at the persons usually branded as deadwood. Almost always they are holdovers from once powerful but now defeated factions. They often aren't really dead in the productive sense; they are stymied. But they are treated as good as dead by those in the currently winning faction, who are not about to give them a shot at advancement unless it involves an inordinately high risk of failure. Corollary Fifteen:

Persons labeled as deadwood are usually holdovers, stymied members of defeated factions.

So, to be a privileged member of a winning faction runs a high risk of ultimately becoming deadwood, unless one of two things happens:

• You get promoted to the top while your faction is in power.

• You are able to jump to the rival faction as it takes over.

Notice how powerless you really are. You may not have wanted to join your faction in the first place but did so only to avoid isolation and inevitable failure. You did a good job and worked your way into a privileged position. Now your faction is losing out due to forces over which you have no control, and you can either stay loyally with them and become deadwood or jump ship and be a traitor to your faction. Some deal! But this is precisely the situation in which many rising middle managers find themselves midpoint in their careers.

Dwight, married, forty, with two kids, is in this predicament. He is the auditor of a telephone company in the west. He has held that job for about a year and was recently made assistant vice-president. As is the case in many large corporations, his company is highly bureaucratized, and in fact has a fundamental split in the management—basically between selling and collecting. These are the rival factions.

On one side is marketing. On the other is finance. Dwight, of course, belongs to the latter faction, as does the president of the corporation. But this situation will change in a year and a half, when the president retires and is replaced by one from the rival divison, marketing.

Dwight is highly regarded among the big shots in finance—they know him well from various jobs he's held on their side of the business. But he hasn't had much of anything to do with marketing. They have nothing personally against him—other than that he is in finance—they simply don't know him. Dwight has been given the nod by his faction for a promotion to vice president. The job will open up when the current vice president retires, but he has not yet decided to take early retirement. If he does, he will leave before the new president takes over. This would be very good for Dwight. His faction will certainly back him for the promotion, and the rival faction has no reason to scream its collective heads off about it—yet.

But they soon may have. An audit of the marketing department was routinely given to Dwight, the auditor, to look over and okay. But the audit was packed with bad news for marketing—a whole series of very damaging revelations, all of which centered around the bad choices of the senior vice president of that division. This man is the best friend of the next president of the corporation. None of the findings showed dishonesty or illegality, but they revealed a staggering negligence and incompetence that could and maybe even should end this guy's career.

The usual procedure, after an internal audit, is to show it to everybody and anybody in the company who's willing to look at it, but few are usually interested. If it doesn't contain any dirt, who cares? The auditor has two options:

- He can send it out without changing a fact or figure.

- He can doctor it. This doesn't involve a cover-up, naturally. But auditors have ways to group and categorize that can make the embezzlements of Fulgencio Batista look like contributions to the United Way.

So Dwight's problem is straightforward. He can doctor the audit and thus not outrage the marketing faction, or he can send it out without change and outrage them, but bring smiles to the faces of his allies in finance. There would be no contest; he would simply go with his own guys, except he has to consider the possibility of a promotion before the new president takes over, or after. If he makes the wrong choice he's deadwood.

Dwight applied the Basic Decision-making Principle of Game Theory to his two choices:

"If I don't doctor the audit, and the current vice president doesn't retire until the new president takes over, I'm screwed. I think my career here would be stymied. I wouldn't be fired, I just wouldn't get anywhere, no matter what I did. To advance my career, I'd have to leave the company, which would be a shame after all the time I've put into it.

"If I doctor the audit, which I've given a lot of thought to doing, what I don't want but am afraid I might get is that the current vice president *will* retire early. My pals in finance might get wind of the original report—remember a junior auditor did it, and those guys sometimes talk. My buddies, who have backed me all these years, would feel let down, betrayed. This would kill my promotion—they'd promote somebody else, that's for sure. Then, if I'm passed over by my own faction, I surely won't be promoted by the rival one later. Anyway, there would be nothing to promote me into because the V.P. job would have already been filled. So I'd be both deadwood and a traitor. This would be worse."

Dwight's best strategy is to issue the report as is: "Screw that jerk from marketing. I just hope that V.P. decides to move to Catalina soon."

The Basic Decision-making Principle of Game Theory allowed Dwight to evaluate his temptation to jump factions. He saw clearly that his best interests were in taking his chances with his present faction. To an outsider, Dwight might have appeared to be acting out of the loyalty of a stalwart. And he was, for his own personal gain.

There are several lessons from Game Theory in this chapter:

- **Middle manager loners are virtually doomed to failure.**

- **To get to the top, you must join a faction, whether you want to or not.**

- **Time is the catch. Factions gain and lose power.**

- **If your faction loses, you could become dead-wood.**

- **You can use the Basic Decision-making Principle of Game Theory to evaluate whether or not to switch factions.**

Part 7
Bargaining

44

The Walkaway Point vs. The Standard Promotional Formula

TO DETERMINE WHETHER A compromise is worth the effort in a way that is emotionally satisfying, one needs either very good intuition or a system. This chapter will provide a system.

What we are looking for is a *walkaway point:* the point at which you decide an offered or existing deal is not as good for you as walking away from it.

What's so critical about knowing your walkaway point? Without it you are always at the mercy of the other guy. If he realizes that you'll keep backing up, he may keep pushing. But if there is a point where you will no longer participate in the deal, then there is a limit to how far he can push. He is understandably concerned about not losing the deal or he wouldn't be trying to make it. So he is also always trying to figure out your walkaway point, and if he senses that you don't know what it is, he'll also figure you for a pushover. This brings us to Corollary Sixteen:

The single most important point in any office politics agreement is the point at which you walk away from it.

When would you reject a deal as unsatisfactory? One situation would certainly be when you have a better offer. Then you take the better offer. Corollary Seventeen:

At some point in any negotiation, if the other party asks for too much, or offers you too little, you always have a better offer.

This is because, at some point, no deal is better than a bad deal, and no deal is your better offer. The only question is, how do you determine that point? Ask yourself: If I turn down this offer, what is it I don't want but am afraid I might get? If you use this simple test, you'll be amazed at how many bum deals you'll reject and how good you'll feel about it. This question establishes your walkaway point. It is absolutely nonnegotiable. How could it be? You didn't make a deal with anyone to get it. This is what you can do entirely on your own.

We have applied the Basic Decision-making Principle of Game Theory in many examples, and have never obtained a hard and fast numerical value. Isn't a firm value necessary as a walkaway point? No. As we shall see, the application of the Basic Decision-making Principle will do the job. Of course, if you can come up with an absolute number, so much the better, providing you stick with it. Having confidence in an absolute number is tough to do; it requires a detailed foresight that few of us have.

Once you realize that you have a walkaway point that is nonnegotiable, you can appreciate another basic concept of bargaining, Corollary Eighteen:

Everything is negotiable except your walkaway point.

Absolutely everything else, without exception. The reason is simple. The only truth you know in the bargain is how you feel about your walkaway point. Everything else is an offer or a claim from some other guy. His claim may be true or false. It may be verbal or in writing. It may be on embossed stationery with notary public stamps all over it. It may be page 26, paragraph 3 of the corporation's book of procedures. And it may be a bluff. If you have a clear walkaway point, you can test it.

A test case of this is the standard promotional formula used by many corporations and nonprofit institutions. An example from the latter is particularly relevant here for several reasons:

- Administrators of a nonprofit organization will almost always claim that they can't even afford to pay the raise called for by the standard promotional formula. (Executives at a private corporation will rarely make this claim. It suggests they aren't successful.)

- The myth of the nonprofit sector is that it is more bureaucratized than the for-profit sector. Thus written procedures allegedly carry more weight there than in organizations motivated totally by greed.

- Administrators in the nonprofit sector will often try to lecture you on the public service of the organization and thus shame you into asking for less than you otherwise would: "We're not here for the money, we're here to do public service." There may even be a grain of truth in the claim, but it is inevitably, and sometimes only, made when you are up for a raise. It's a claim that would never be made in private enterprise, where everybody is in it for the money and nobody pretends otherwise. The equivalent claim in private enterprise is simply *wait*.

Anita, thirty, was promoted from unit manager to divisional coordinator in a health-care administration facility in San Francisco. She received the official letter of promotion, but there was a slight hitch over salary. She checked around at comparable institutions and found that she should expect a raise of $3000 to $7000 over her present pay. This is what divisional coordinators were getting at other institutions, so she figured this is what market forces were determining—except in her case. She was informed that she'd get only a $1500 increase. When she asked what was up, she was told by the V.P. of administration that there was a standard promotional formula for anybody who already worked at the organization. He pulled out the book of pro-

cedures and showed her the relevant section. There it was in
bold type: $1500.

She went home to think it over and decided to work out her
walkaway point. To do so she listed her options:

- She could agree to the offer—the promotion and the
  $1500.

- She could turn down the offer unless they sweetened the
  terms considerably. By how much, she wasn't sure, but
  at least to somewhere in the middle of the $3000 to
  $7000 range. In the meantime, while they were hag-
  gling—*if* they were haggling—she'd look around for another job.

- She could quit the job.

Anita then applied the Basic Decision-making Principle of
Game Theory to figure out her walkaway point:

"If I agree to the offer as is, what I don't want but am afraid I
might get is that I'll feel like a jerk. This job has a lot more responsibility, and so it should be more money. If they hired somebody from outside, they'd have to pay more. I don't want to live
my life feeling like a doormat. So this option is out.

"If I turn down the offer unless they sweeten it to somewhere in the middle of the $3000 to $7000 range, what I don't
want but am afraid I might get is that they won't improve it, or
not by enough. Then I'll have to think about leaving this institution. But they've already said I'm qualified to be a divisional
coordinator by offering me the job, so I'm in a position to make a
strong case with another medical institution. This isn't so bad.

"If I quit, my pride is assuaged, but what I don't want but
am afraid I might get is that my rent won't be paid, so this isn't
very good."

Anita's best strategy was to turn down the offer unless they
sweetened it and to look around for another job. Her walkaway
point in any possible negotiation was somewhere in the middle
of the $3000 to $7000 range.

She went back to the V.P. of administration and turned
down the offer unless he improved the salary. Since she had already decided to leave the institution, she figured she'd lose
nothing by asking for a $7000 increase, the maximum she had
heard about. Anita expected the V.P. to say something like, "I'm
sorry, but we have to stick with the salary guidelines." So she
nearly fell off her chair when he said, "We can't offer that much,
but I'll get back to you with something." So much for the standard promotional formula! It was a bluff. The administration
was simply trying to bulldoze her with that printed relic of some
administrator's flimflam. Isn't it amazing how nice people can
sometimes be such bullies?

He offered her $2500. She turned it down flat, asking in-
stead for $6000. He rejected that, but came back to her two days
later with his "final" offer: $4500. This wasn't quite the mid-
point of the $3000 to $7000 range, falling $500 short, so she
evaluated it using the Basic Decision-making Principle:

"If I turn down this offer, what I don't want but am afraid I
might get is all the trouble of looking for another job.

"If I take the offer, what I don't want but am afraid I might
get is to lose out on a possible extra $500. It's suddenly obvious
that avoiding the trouble of looking for another job is easily
worth the $500 hypothetical difference."

She took the offer and felt very good about it.

This situation presents a standard bargaining process. Anita
first found out the comparable salary ranges of other institutions. She figured that the V.P. of administration would also
know these salaries. The midpoint in such a range is a prominent
settlement point. She then established her walkaway point at
"somewhere in the middle" of the range by applying the Basic
Decision-making Principle. She was able to make her decision to
accept what he said was his final offer by using a second application of the Basic Decision-making Principle to see if the offer
was above her walkaway point. She was best able to determine
this at the moment when she was confronted with the choice,
not in an armchair manner beforehand. This is why setting an ar-

bitrary numerical walkaway point is not always wise. A little vagueness in your own mind is sometimes better.

She could have pressed a bit more, but his offer was acceptable; she had wanted to stay rather than change jobs, and he had made significant improvements in his offer. She would have to work with him in the future and was reluctant to run the risk of creating a tense working relationship. For an agreement to be stable, both parties have to be satisfied with it, not only intellectually but emotionally. If Anita had pushed too hard, the V.P. may have felt had, and might have taken it out on her in subtle ways. Anita, of course, never made any attempt to figure out his walkaway point, so she had no way of knowing.

Notice that the V.P. knew something about Anita's walkaway point. He had probably expected her to take his initial offer, and he was now trying to guess her salary minimum, but her walkaway point wasn't a specific sum. It was the decision to look for another job unless he made her a deal comparable to what she could get elsewhere. Eventually the V.P. crossed the critical threshold. Anita probably couldn't have said in advance exactly where the threshold was, but by using the Basic Decision-making Principle of Game Theory a second time she could tell if he had crossed it. It helped her to get closer to her own feelings; and this gave her the strength to proceed.

There are several lessons from Game Theory in this chapter:

- **The most important strength you have in any agreement is a clear understanding of when you should walk away from it.**

- **You can use the Basic Decision-making Principle of Game Theory to establish your walkaway point.**

- **Everything is negotiable except your walkaway point. Everything includes all office procedures, even if chiseled in the marble walls of the office vestibule.**

- **Your walkaway point does not have to be a specific number. It can be a limited range. The precise**

value of it can be determined in the course of negotiation by a second application of the Basic Decision-making Principle.

45

Keeping the Boss Guessing About Your Walkaway Strategy

STANDARD PROMOTIONAL FORMULAS ALSO exist in private enterprise. They are more difficult for top management to defend
with a straight face than they are in the nonprofit sector. But
since top management in private enterprise got where it is, at
least to some extent, by keeping a straight face, executives are all
too often able to bully their subordinates into not asking for
much of anything. As a consequence their explanations for denial are not always as elegant or lengthy as in the not-for-profit
sector. Some typical explanations offered by senior management
for keeping their foot on your neck:

- *Promotions are too frequent in this company.* There is a
  remote hint of intellectual depth to this remark—executive inflation, comparable to grade inflation in academia,
  or just plain inflation.

- *I get paid according to the number of subordinates I
  have. Why would I want to promote you out of my department?* Although it's hard to believe anyone would

actually say this, as opposed to practicing it, several persons at different companies have reported the remark to me.

- *I don't think you've proved to me yet that you're worth more money.*

- **No!**

This chapter will deal with a way to handle all of these objections before they are raised. The important question to ask yourself is this: What is the goal of the negotiation? If you say, "I win; I get the raise," you've given the wrong answer. We are dealing with bargaining, and the essence of any bargain not backed by a gun is expressed in Corollary Nineteen:

Both parties must feel better off with the deal than without it.

In other words, both of you have to feel that you've won. Unless you can get your boss to view your promotion this way, you probably won't get it. So you have to ask yourself, "What can he gain from my getting promoted?" If, after racking your brain for a few days, you decide there is nothing at all in it for him, you may be in trouble. But there usually is something. A few examples:

- A subordinate who doesn't quit on him at a critical moment.

- A subordinate who will back him up far and wide in the company, telling everybody what a great guy he is.

- An ally in another department, which is what he could have you promoted into.

- Somebody he'll feel freer to dump more work onto.

- A hatchet man.

The list could go on, and you might not feel terrific about some of the items, but this is the sort of list you should draw up to see if there is something you can find that appeals to the boss. Once you've found it, be careful. It must be expressed to him very subtly. Corollary Twenty:

Never tell the boss what's good for him.

For proof of this, apply the Basic Decision-making Principle of Game Theory. If you tell him, what you don't want but very likely will get is his resentment. You're forcing him to acknowledge to you that you know the politics of his job better than he does. You are also forcing him to acknowledge that he is promoting you not exclusively on the merit of your work but because there is something in it for him. He might piously accuse you of "deal-making," which is precisely what you are doing, and which he is only too happy to do also, providing he doesn't have to admit it. If you don't tell him outright, what you don't want but are afraid you might get is that you were too subtle and he didn't get it. You can always try again with slightly less indirection.

From this we can conclude Corollary Twenty-one:

Asking for a raise or a promotion is simply one portion of making a deal with the boss. The other portion is asking yourself what he gets in return.

To treat the issue of getting a raise and/or promotion as deal-making, you should try to figure out a number of its key elements:

- your walkaway point
- his walkaway point
- what he gets out of it

- your net gain from the deal, considering that he's going to have to get something, too

- a subtle way to communicate to him what he gets out of it, without appearing to communicate it. This is your bargaining strategy.

While you're bargaining you don't want to tip off the other person to your walkaway point. If he knows, that's all he has to offer you. The idea is to get him to figure it out and hope that in the process he overshoots it. On the other hand, you can sometimes get a pretty good idea of your boss's walkaway point. How? The constraints under which he operates may be apparent to you in the course of your work. This could put you in a favored position if you are bargaining for a raise and promotion.

Les, thirty, married, with one kid, was in this position. He was definitely on the fast track at his company, a major money center bank that we'll call Big Bank, Inc. Hired as a CPA, within a year he was made a manager in the accounting department. After a few months in his new position, he was put in charge of his own staff, composed of three managers and four assistant managers. Not bad for less than two years on the job. During this same period he completed an MBA degree at night. Les was in daily touch with senior V.P.s because his staff was given particularly tough jobs, at which they excelled. Les, who came from a lower-middle-class Armenian background, was definitely not from Harvard, Wharton, or Stanford, but he was beginning to be considered for admission into the main faction.

This would require a rapid promotion to assistant vice president. Les needed the promotion. Without it, he would lose his fast-track standing, which he had worked so hard to achieve. He also needed the psychological lift a promotion would give him. He had come from nowhere, he felt, and this would put him someplace. He also needed the money. He had received marvelous evaluations, and so was sure to get a merit increase. But that would be $6000 less than the increase he would get if promoted to assistant vice president.

In addition, he had been a de facto assistant vice president for the past year. There was a vacancy and he had taken up the slack.

Confident that he was worthy of promotion to assistant V.P., he gingerly broached the topic with the vice president in charge of accounting policy, a gentleman with whom Les had always gotten along, but from a social distance. Les indicated that he hoped to get his promotion at his next annual review. This is when the V.P. dropped the bomb. He had instituted his own standard promotional formula: Every manager would have to hold that job for at least two years before getting a shot at a promotion to assistant V.P. Although the thought flashed across Les's mind, he didn't allow himself to dwell on the possibility that the entirely new promotional policy had been instituted to keep an Armenian from getting ahead. As Les put it, "So much of what you bring to the table in any situation is what you have in your mind. I couldn't let this concern over prejudice shape my thinking. I was going for the promotion and that was that. I put that prejudice business someplace else and barged ahead." He was going to get his promotion, policy or no policy. But this required that he plan it.

At the same time, other areas of Big Bank began to court him, hinting at a promotion to their area, sounding him out. He had no idea if they would actually follow through with an offer, but he decided he'd better work out his bargaining strategy before doing anything else. First he worked out his walkaway point, based on what he saw as his two options: Slug it out at the bank or move on to greener pastures.

"If I slug it out, what I don't want but am afraid I might get is not get promoted in time to stay on the fast track. That would be lousy. I'd be better off leaving the bank. I've been offered other jobs but at smaller banks.

"But if I go to another bank, what I don't want but am afraid I might get is to find out later through my contacts that I was about to get the promotion. This is just as bad as staying and not getting the promotion. Either way I lose my fast-track status."

In short, unlike Anita in our previous chapter, Les did not have a clear-cut best strategy. He was rationally torn between alternatives. Since this was the case, he decided he might as well adopt it as his walkaway strategy: He should be undecided about staying or leaving, and he should let everyone know it.

Being undecided is effectively the same as keeping one's strategy secret. Recall that this is one of the key concepts in dueling. Les was not involved in an office duel, but he could borrow one of the concepts from dueling if appropriate. It was very much to the point in this case, because Les did not want the V.P. to know what he was up to. Why not? If the V.P. knew Les would stay, no matter what, he didn't have to give him the promotion. And if Les said outright that he'd leave or else, the V.P. could get his back up and say, "Fine, go ahead."

Notice that there are two bargaining concepts from Game Theory:

- **The walkaway point.** Although Les's walkaway point was clear—losing his fast-track status—the walkaway point can also be defined as you go along. After checking the market for your services, apply the Basic Decision-making Principle of Game Theory to find both a realistic and an acceptable range of possible offers. Any offer less than the range should be rejected. If necessary, apply the principle a second time to evaluate a specific offer if you're not sure whether to accept or reject it. This is what Anita did in the previous chapter.

- **The walkaway strategy.** This is either your best strategy, developed using the Basic Decision-making Principle of Game Theory, or if there isn't a clear-cut best strategy, it is the strategy of being unpredictable.

Les's walkaway point was poor. What he didn't want but was afraid he might get—losing his fast-track standing at a major bank—occurred with either of his options. But the V.P. didn't know this, and Les was not going to let him know. He was going to keep it secret by adopting the walkaway strategy of being un-predictable.

Next, Les tried to figure out the V.P.'s walkaway point. He did this by asking himself a simple question: If I left the bank, what is it the V.P. doesn't want but is afraid he might get?

He decided there were three things that the V.P. wouldn't want:

1. He would lose specialized accounting knowledge that Les had but no one else in the department did.

2. He would lose a manager who was known by top management to be very effective, and was in fact the manager of more than half the staff in the department.

3. He would lose an effective manager with a CPA, an MBA, and eight years of business experience, who was on the fast track.

Les didn't know exactly how this would add up in the V.P.'s mind, but he didn't think that losing Les would look good for him. He could get another manager and find somebody else with Les's specialized technical knowledge. But losing such an effective manager might not sit very well with the vice president's own superiors, especially since he'd be losing Les for no apparent reason. So Les figured the V.P.'s walkaway point was also pretty poor. Of course, Les knew enough not to tell him that. That would be indiscreet and hint at deal-making, which is publicly decried as immoral by those who do it. Besides, he figured the V.P. already knew his own walkaway point. In fact, this analysis made Les think that the V.P.'s announcement of his own standard promotional formula was done either without thinking the consequences through or as a crass attempt to bully Les.

The next question was, what would the V.P. win by promoting Les? After some reflection Les decided that the V.P.'s gain would come from essentially one element—a loyal ally and supporter who might become prominent in the bank. Could Les live with this? If he struck this deal with the V.P., he'd have to, or be branded by others as a man who couldn't be counted on. Les decided, after some soul-searching over the V.P.'s suspected prejudice against Armenians, that he had no other choice than to live with this or not get his promotion. "I don't have to socialize with the bastard, but I do have to speak up for him when necessary," Les told me.

The only thing left was to figure out how to subtly communicate the deal to the V.P. Because Les understood that he should never tell the boss what's good for him (Corollary Twenty), he had to figure out some other way to bargain for the raise. Les chose to try bargaining through the grapevine. Providing he was subtle and didn't violate Corollary Twenty, Les could bargain any way he wanted, or any way he was comfortable with, or any way that was available to him. Corollary Twenty-two:

If you are trying to make a deal with someone who belongs to a faction that you don't belong to, you can bargain any way you like, providing you don't appear to be bargaining.

Les immediately began flooding the grapevine with two stories. One was that he wasn't sure whether or not to take the job offers from other banks he had been receiving. This was Les's walkaway strategy. Everyone believed he might have received offers because it was known that other departments in Big Bank were interested in him. The other story was to the effect that the V.P. was a great guy and brilliant administrator for whom Les had tremendous respect, and especially that Les would "really put himself on the line for this guy." This was Les's offer to the V.P. He told both stories to enough people to practically guarantee that they got back to both the V.P. and the V.P.'s superiors.

The result? Within a few weeks Les's V.P. called him aside and told him that he had reconsidered and that Les would get his promotion to assistant vice president at the next annual review. The bargain was struck and everybody gained. Les got ahead, and the V.P. was able to feel he had a loyal ally in the department. What about his new standard promotional policy? Nothing more was ever heard of it.

There are a number of lessons from Game Theory in this chapter:

- **Don't be bullied by standard promotional formulas. In your case there need be no such thing.**

- **In any agreement not backed by a gun, both parties must feel better off with the deal than without it. Both parties must feel they have won.**

- **Always ask yourself what your boss stands to gain from your promotion.**

- **Never tell your boss what is good for him.**

- **Asking for a promotion or raise is simply making a deal with the boss, and as with any other deal, all the elements must be in place:**

  * **your walkaway point**

  * **his walkaway point**

  * **what he gets out of the deal**

  * **what you get out of it, taking into account what he gets**

  * **your bargaining strategy, which had better be subtle.**

- **You can have a walkaway strategy as well as a walkaway point. A walkaway strategy is either your best strategy, developed using the Basic Decision-making Principle of Game Theory, or if there isn't a clear-cut best strategy, it is the strategy of being unpredictable. The walkaway point is either a specific item, such as Les's losing his fast-track standing, or a range of possible agreements, as with Anita in the previous chapter. The walkaway** point can also be defined as you go along by applying the Basic Decision-making Principle to specific offers that you receive to see if they are good enough.

• You should try to estimate the other guy's walkaway point by applying the Basic Decision-making Principle of Game Theory to him.

• If you are trying to make a deal with someone who belongs to a faction that you don't, you can bargain any way you like, providing you don't appear to be bargaining.

46

When You Are Trapped in an Overspecialized Career Because Your Walkaway Point Is Too High

YOU WANT A BETTER situation at your job, but your boss gains nothing by giving it to you. Furthermore, you can't threaten to walk away because he knows that you can't walk away to anything better. You might still be able to pull a rabbit out of a hat and come up with an agreement that gives you what you want, but the path to it will not be obvious from the situation. To find it requires imagination and a careful analysis of all of the factors involved in a possible bargain. Game Theory shows how to convert a single-factor negotiation where you can't make a deal into a multi-factor one where you can.

Russ, twenty-six, married, no kids, was in this spot. He was an insurance broker with one of the largest brokerage houses in the country, headquartered in San Francisco. The company had sunk three years of training in him in one of the most specialized areas of insurance. It was a very good investment. Russ turned out to be a super salesman. With bonuses he had almost tripled his income in a single year and now had more clients and bigger ones than six other brokers in his area. Russ, in short, was a hotshot, and the company very much wanted to reward him for it with a promotion to assistant vice president. He had just been told to expect the promotion, along with a healthy pay increase, the next month.

So what was his problem? Russ was no dope and had taken a look at his line of business. Although the pay was good, and the promotions were coming, there were certain drawbacks:

1. *His specialized area constituted less than one percent of all insurance sold.* So although his promotional opportunities were good at the moment, the hotshots who counted in his company would almost certainly come from other areas, such as property and casualty insurance, which made up about 70 percent of the insurance sold by his company.

2. *Russ might have to wait in a very slow line for further promotion.* His boss was only twenty-nine, and his boss in turn was thirty-one. Of course, Russ might outshine both of them, but if the two of them worked together, they could almost certainly prevent that.

3. *After the increase Russ's salary would be relatively high for a man his age.* Other insurance brokerage houses might not want to match it, especially considering his very narrow expertise.

After Russ made up this list he practically ran to his bosses and asked that he be allowed to expand his area of activity to include property and casualty insurance. They turned him down flat, arguing that the company had spent too much in getting him where he was. They argued that during his proposed new training, his sales were bound to go down in his specialized area, rather than continue to grow at his usual rate. But Russ suspected that they really were saying something else: "This would make you more mobile. What would you need us for?" because it was precisely the reason that he wanted to start selling the other kind of insurance.

Russ decided it was time to work out his walkaway point. He concluded that he had only two options: to stay or resign. He applied the Basic Decision-making Principle of Game Theory:

"If I leave, what I don't want but am afraid I might get is a huge cut in pay if I go into the property and casualty area at another company, or at most I'll get the same pay if I'm hired to specialize in my present area, in which case, what's the point in changing jobs? Either way is bad.

"If I stay, what I don't want but am afraid I might get is good money in a dead-end job. But for the time being this is better."

So Russ found himself in a peculiar situation: His walkaway strategy was to *stay* at his job. Since he was angling for something better at his company, this didn't give him much leverage. It wasn't great if he was to look for a job at another insurance brokerage house either. He was a most successful broker in a very specialized line of insurance. The other brokerage houses would have a pretty good idea how much he was making. To change he'd have to take a big cut in money. The odd employer might find this courageous and admirable, but a lot of them would just think he was a sap. They might hire him, but might not respect him.

So Russ tried to figure out the brokerage house's walkaway point. He asked himself, "If I left, what is it the company doesn't want but is afraid it might get?"

The answer, unfortunately, was very little. Ninety percent of the revenue from his thirty clients came from exactly six of them, all huge companies. It was extremely unlikely that he would be able to take these principal accounts with him, because although Russ was a good salesman, he represented a very big brokerage house. Big was likely to stick with big. Russ was beginning to feel like a very little man pulling down a disproportionately big salary.

This was Russ's situation: He was trying to strike a bargain with his company in which there was absolutely nothing in it for the company, and in which he had absolutely no leverage. Normally, this would be the end of the story. But Russ kept at it. He went back to his boss and offered to give up all but the top six of his accounts if he were allowed to expand into the other lines of insurance. This was reasonable from Russ's point of view because his salary was based on his account list, and this would keep his income at something approaching its present level. Also, the top six companies used up about 90 percent of his time. So this would give him some time for training in property and casualty. But again the company turned him down flat. Why should the company concede anything? They already had all of the accounts, and turning over the smaller ones to some other guy meant nothing to the bosses.

Russ had figured out the company's walkaway point, and this had so far done him no good, so he now tried to figure out what the company might want out of a possible new deal. He made up a list of possibilities:

- Not to pay the promotional salary if they were going to lose him eventually. The company was willing, even eager, to pay him a promotional salary if they knew he would stay. They weren't crooks, they were just protecting themselves.

- Russ's loyalty and continued employment with the company.

- A person trained in Russ's specialized area.

- Not to lose his current sales growth while training him in property and casualty insurance.

Russ's problem was that he had viewed this bargain as a single-factor negotiation. But this list revealed that a number of key factors were involved in this deal, and if Russ were to get his promotion and new training, he would have to deal with enough of them to make the company happy. The bosses had already acknowledged Russ's current sales growth, and although they hadn't mentioned it, he was keenly aware they were worried about losing him. In short, the bosses were concerned about future contingencies. This should hardly have surprised Russ, since that is what insurance is all about. Corollary Twenty-three:

Contingency arrangements can often be used to resolve a wide range of bargaining problems, which could not be resolved by haggling over a single issue. Contingency agreements can convert a single-factor deal into a multi-factor one.

Russ then went back to the bosses with another offer, which was a bit complicated, but quite interesting: He would still get the promotion, but would not immediately collect the pay increase that went with it. This would be accrued, with interest, over two years. The amount to be paid him would depend on a continued growth of his specialized portfolio by 20 percent per month, which was his rate of sales growth. He would assure that growth by helping to train and phase in his replacement while the company trained him in property and casualty insurance. If the growth of his portfolio dropped below 20 percent per month, on an annual average, his accrued pay increase would be proportionately decreased. In the event that he left within the two-year period, he would forfeit the accrued amount. He would, of course, earn his regular commissions on his current portfolio and on whatever he sold in the property and casualty area.

His proposal met virtually all of the bosses' requirements, and they went for the deal. Incidentally, top management was impressed by Russ's imagination, perseverance, and bargaining ability. He's now clumping the corridors with the big boys.

There are several lessons from Game Theory in this chapter:

- An analysis of your walkaway point may reveal that you have no incentive to leave your job. Your walkaway strategy may be to stay. In effect, you may be bound with golden chains. This, of course, leaves you with no leverage for bargaining for a better deal with your company.

- An analysis may show that the company doesn't get much out of a new job arrangement with you. They may have no incentive to give you anything.

- You should then analyze what the company might want to get out of any possible agreement with you.

- Using a contingency agreement, you may be able to satisfy the company's and your own wants.

When You Have to Enforce a Standard Promotional Formula or Face a Rebellion in Your Department

BOSSES, TOO, CAN BE victimized by a standard promotional formula. They may not have created the policy, but may be in the unpleasant position of having to enforce it. Even worse, they may see the total folly of the policy, but have very little room to do anything about it. So they get caught in the middle, which is of course the definition of a middle manager: a manager caught in the middle.

Often this dilemma can be resolved by a variation of the technique described in the previous chapter: turning a single-issue negotiation into a multi-issue one. Sometimes this will bring new parties into the bargain, and they can be used to find a settlement. When this can be accomplished, rabbits can be pulled out of hats.

Jody, thirty-three, divorced, one child, pulled off this minor miracle. She is an assistant vice president at corporate headquarters of a large Dallas insurance company. Her department is financial control, and she "runs" it, or rather she enforces corporate policy in it, which means more or less that it runs her. She does, however, have certain discretionary powers—hiring, firing, and promotions, within the corporate standard promotional formula.

Accordingly, she hired Ely right after he graduated from an MBA program at a prestigious Texas university. Ely had gone directly from a BA in political science to the MBA program to this job as a junior financial analyst. This was his first job. He turned out to be very good, a real go-getter. He established a good working relationship with the various divisional controllers, virtually all of whom phoned Jody to tell her how good he was, and also took charge of several proposals for the corporate controller. He took it upon himself to stay late and work weekends to institute a computerized data base for Jody's department. This speeded up the production of statistical summaries tremendously, for which Jody received a large number of compliments. Ely accomplished all of this in about eight months. There was no question that the guy was good, especially in his own mind.

He wanted a payoff, right away. He wanted to be promoted to assistant manager when he had been at the company one full year, which would also be one full year ahead of the time spelled out in the standard promotional formula. When he was hired Jody and her boss, a V.P., had explained the conditions of the job, and Ely had bought it at the time. There was little else he could do if he wanted the job. But three weeks before, Ely had asked Jody and her boss the date of his promotion. They had reminded him of the company's standard promotional formula, and that seemed to do it until a week ago. Ely met with Jody again to discuss his promotion and told her point-blank that he might very well look for another job if he didn't get his promotion, pronto.

This guy knew about walkaway strategies, but this put Jody in a double bind. Ely had made himself known as a promising employee to an awful lot of higher-ups. So if he left Jody would have to explain why. This would be awkward because the company had made a big deal about getting great MBA holders and giving them a chance to excel. It especially didn't want to train them in the ins and outs of its practices and then watch them defect to rival insurance companies. Jody would take the rap.

So she brought it up with her boss, the V.P. "Absolutely not! Ely can wait just like everybody else does here," the V.P. told her. Jody was caught by a standard promotional formula.

If this weren't enough, the other members of her department got wind of Ely's attempt to catapult ahead, and they weren't happy about it. All of them had either an MBA or a CPA. Several came up to Jody and complained about how they had put in their time, and "how come this guy thinks he can just come right in here and take over?" Jody had the beginnings of a rebellion on her hands. She was definitely caught in the middle.

She was pretty sure she knew Ely's walkaway point: He'd make a run for it if he didn't get a promotion soon. And she'd been told her walkaway strategy: No. If she tried to convince her boss to change her walkaway strategy, she'd have a lot of unhappy people working for her. Not much room for bargaining, was there? No matter what she did, she'd be in trouble. Maybe. She made a list of her problems:

- She was blocked from promoting Ely.

- She would be blamed if he quit.

- If she went to bat for him, the other persons who worked for her would scream.

- Ely was a guy champing at the bit for more and greater responsibilities, and he had a wide range of abilities, including computer skills.

When you're stuck in a bargaining problem, always make a list such as this. A solution will often reveal itself. The last item on Jody's list pointed her in the right direction. Ely was blocked from a promotion in his department. How about promoting him into another department? He had been extremely successful at everything he had done. Why not go outside the department to add to his responsibilities? Jody couldn't transfer him because that would look as if she didn't want him in her department, which wasn't true. But she could lend him to data management, which badly needed him to help them set up a new computer system. The V.P. in charge of data management was very happy about the loan, and was even willing to pay the price Jody insisted on; assuming Ely did well on the new computer system project, the V.P. would recommend him for early promotion. The irate rebels couldn't really complain. All of them had been offered a chance to work on the new system and had turned it down. Ely, of course, grabbed it.

Every objection had been answered. If Jody's V.P. had objected to the promotion when it came up—which wasn't likely since the V.P.'s peer was asking for it—Ely would simply have been transferred to data management.

Jody's V.P. didn't object, and Ely got the promotion.

The bargaining principle involved here is expressed in Corollary Twenty-four:

If you expand the bargain to include a wider range of settlements, you might be able to bring new bargainers into the deal, and they may loosen up the constraints.

The V.P. in charge of data management was an example.

There are several lessons from Game Theory in this chapter:

- You may have your walkaway strategy imposed on you from above.

- A hotshot subordinate may make his walkaway strategy crystal clear to you.

- There may be no room for bargaining as things stand.

- If you expand the bargain to include a wider range of settlements, you might be able to bring new big shots into the deal, and they may loosen up the constraints. If you do this right, the new guys will not be the boss of your boss but his peers.

48

When You Want to Set Up Your Own Business but Must Use Your Present Job as a Springboard

OF COURSE YOU GET up in the morning, go to work, perform the requirements of the job, perhaps quite well, collect your paycheck and bonuses, and maybe even get promoted on the fast track. Is this what you identify as your true work in life? Maybe not. While researching this book, I talked to an amazing number of people who are doing something else, usually on the sly, which is what they consider their *real* careers.

Imagine a large corporation, say a huge bank in which absolutely nobody, from president to tellers and including the guards, actually believes that he or she works at the bank as a career. What do they really do? The president is running for governor or angling for a cabinet job in Washington. The senior vice presidents want to become presidents of one of the large manufacturing corporations or conglomerates that are clients of the bank. The assistant vice presidents are getting MBAs so they can change their careers altogether. The auditors are quietly setting up their own public accounting firms on the side and are already making a sizable bundle during tax season. The tellers are going to night school to learn court reporting. The bank guard has been buying rural property on an obscure lake which he plans to turn into a fishing pond for tourists. Nobody really works for the bank.

If you go to their offices and ask any of these people what they do, they naturally will tell you the job that gives them their paychecks. But if you ask them away from work, with no witnesses and no tape recorders, they'll tell you what they really *believe* they do. The only way they can take the unpleasantness out of their paying job is to believe they do something else, and the job delivering the paycheck is just a temporary expedient, a high-paying back-up job.

After researching this book, I suspect that what I found is characteristic of corporate America: The overwhelming bulk of the American economy may be living the myth of the emperor's clothes. *Virtually nobody believes that he really does what he publicly appears to be doing.*

I know this is hard to accept, and I'm still not absolutely convinced of it myself, but it seems to be more true than false. Consider a select list of occupations contrasted with what the holders of those occupations often actually believe they do:

accountants ..... entrepreneurial tycoons
actors .... real estate magnates
artists .... real estate tycoons

dentists	tennis pros, real estate magnates
doctors	stockbrokers, business executives
lawyers	actors, novelists
real estate	
tycoons	Broadway producers
screen-	
writers	directors, stock-market portfolio analysts
stockbrokers	screenwriters, novelists
middle	
managers	anything else

Everybody thinks he's some other guy. Of course, not all of us are acting on these hidden occupations. The point is that most persons in your corporation are not emotionally committed to what they are doing. Here are some reasons:

Most major corporations are now diversified. If one could have once believed in the products, now the corporation is organized by strategic business units, which are planted, grown, and harvested. You know that the days of any product are numbered. The only constant is the portfolio of businesses. It's hard to invest one's emotions in portfolio analysis, especially of somebody else's portfolio.

Because of takeovers, corporate identities are constantly being lost. People train in one company, only to have it swallowed up by another. Half the managers are sacked. The ones who remain are in daily fear that they'll be next and are constantly being menaced by what they often see as a new clump of arrogant idiots from corporate. As likely as not, the new bosses have decided to "harvest" the company—in other words, bleed it. If you're a member of the elite corp of slashers and burners, you might have a guilty conscience and tell yourself that you really do something else for a living.

Big corporations don't even stick to their own names. EXXON. EXXON? What was it before?

What about the company men who really look, act, and talk

as if they believe in the company? They especially may not believe in what they're doing. They're clumpers, and what you see
is simply the disguise of the clump. That way they don't have to
remember to whom they told the truth, since they haven't told it
to anyone. The fact that their every public action seems to indicate total commitment to the company should be taken as the
best evidence to the contrary.

Although few, if any, at your company will admit to not believing in what they do there, they usually give themselves
away. They will do so in many different ways. In talking about
their job, they will often include a few key phrases:

- a means to an end
- a springboard
- another road to Rome
- a good thing to be doing for a while
- I like my work but . . .
- The job has its advantages.
- Don't get me wrong, there are great opportunities here,
  but . . .
- They're using me and I'm using them.
- I'd rather not talk about my job.

You should add to the list by searching for phrases you may
have used that hint at another interest. Then, if you want to
cover that fact, avoid the giveaway phrases. You have to keep
your true plans secret, even if you're not acting on them. If your
thoughts are found out, you'll be either fired or stymied, "de-
clumped" either way because you might loosen someone else's
tongue and blow his cover. And he could be your own boss.

This is precisely the spot Steve, thirty, was in. He worked in
time-buying at a major New York advertising agency. Alfred had
been brought in from a rival agency and made V.P. of the depart-

ment; so he was Steve's boss. Alfred was well known in the industry for doing other people's dirty work, but he was trying to live this down. Steve had complete contempt for Alfred, but he didn't have any vested interest. For the past nine months he had been secretly setting up his own company, and he figured he needed only another six to nine months of steady paychecks. The change of V.P. was somewhat of a setback for Steve. He simply needed a quiet few months of collecting his paychecks so he could get out.

The problem was that Alfred was ambition incarnate. He wanted to be CEO of the company, and to get closer to his goal, he hobnobbed a lot. When he did he wanted to be accompanied by a phalanx of backers, Steve among them. He wanted Steve to clump with him in the corridors, and he had told him so. He literally offered him a deal: "Play the game." If he did, Alfred had implied, Steve could get a better job and more money. If he didn't, he could get fired.

Steve figured out Alfred's walkaway strategy:

"He can fire me or try to get me publicly identified as one of his backers. If he makes me one of his prominent backers, what he doesn't want but is afraid he might get is that I won't be prominent, which is bad for him. But if he fires me or passes me over, what he doesn't want but is afraid he might get is that people will say what a rat he is, passing over or firing a guy just because he didn't hire him. And he can't defend himself by telling the truth, saying something like 'I didn't promote him because he wasn't sleazy enough for me.' So passing me over or firing me are the worst for him. His walkaway strategy is to get me publicly on his side."

What about Steve's walkaway point? He decided he could:

- quit the job

- hang on to the job, but out of sight, hoping to keep it for another six months

- hang on and hobnob, hoping to get more money and less work.

Steve applied the Basic Decision-making Principle of Game Theory to work out his walkaway point:

"If I leave, what I don't want but am afraid I might get is to have to waste my focus searching for another job, which might land me in another bucket of political snakes. I really don't like being in big corporations. A job with a tiny organization would probably mean less money, and that means less money to put into my own company, so this is lousy.

"If I hang in but out of sight, what I don't want but am afraid I might get is that Alfred will can me. That puts me back in the same soup as with the previous choice.

"If I hang in and hobnob, what I don't want but am afraid I might get is to go nuts from the pressure. But I might also get more money from a cushier job, which I could throw into my own company, and this might get me out of here faster. So this is my walkaway strategy."

This analysis reveals an interesting fact. There is no way to tell from a rational man's actions whether he harbors secret plans to dump corporate life or not. His walkaway strategy will be the same either way.

Steve and Alfred made their deal. Steve hung around, publicly showing himself to be Alfred's right-hand man; and Alfred promoted him. Alfred was ambitious but not dishonest. If he implied he would do something he did it. Five months later, Steve quit to work full-time in his own company.

There are several lessons from Game Theory in this chapter:

- **The fact that somebody appears to be a company person doesn't mean he really is. He would have the same walkaway strategy either way.**

- **If you are planning to set up your own company, keep it quiet.**

- **Listen for giveaway phrases. You may not be the only one planning to cut loose from the big corporation.**

49
Negotiating a Performance Appraisal

BEEN TO THE PRIZEFIGHTS lately? You might hate the brutality, but they have an interesting strategic element. Time the rounds, and notice what happens during the last fifteen seconds. If the two contestants in the ring are ever going to try to beat each other's brains out, they'll usually do it during the last fifteen seconds of each round. They do this not out of charity, so each has a chance to be saved by the bell, but to make an impression on the judges.

When a judge is watching the fight, he can't be writing on his scorecard, and vice versa. He can't fairly judge what he doesn't see, so he'll keep his eyes glued to the action. When the round's over and he fills in his scorecard, he'll scratch his head trying to remember what he saw. He can remember quite clearly what he saw most recently, say the last fifteen seconds of each round. Of course, he might remember the whole round, but what he sees at the end will be freshest in his mind, especially if it contains much more energy than did the earlier portion of the round.

A similar phenomenon can occur during the annual or semi-annual supervisors' performance appraisal of subordinates. The subordinates will often go all-out just before the appraisal. This is usually not because they are lazy slobs trying to get a free ride, but because the performance appraisals are usually done with no back-up. In other words, the supervisor usually doesn't have a thick file of many smaller performance appraisals, each covering a specific day, week, or even month. In remembering what happened in the course of the year, he can probably recall what happened this week and maybe last week—unless he has a score to settle. That could have been set in motion many months earlier. So the subordinate's job is to avoid grudge matches with the boss during most of the year. He accomplishes this by working very carefully, steadily, and ploddingly.

Because of these obvious flaws in the annual performance evaluation, many public accounting firms have more or less abandoned annual and semiannual supervisorial evaluations in favor of an immediate evaluation the day after an assignment is completed. Most assignments are only a few days in length, although some can be considerably longer. But by the end of the year there is usually a fat folder of separate appraisals for each subordinate. And he's usually signed each one, and had a conference with the boss and the boss's boss about them. So he always knows what the boss claims in writing about how he's doing. Based on this, he gets an idea of what's expected. Score settling is less likely in this kind of set-up than in an ordinary annual review with no back-up.

The folly of the ordinary annual performance appraisal can be even greater than what I have already described. Sometimes the employee is expected to be dumb enough to criticize himself and even put it in writing. Would you be foolish enough to give anyone a rope to hang you? So if people feel compelled to admit to any weaknesses, they usually try to figure out the blandest possible types of self-criticism.

Supervisors too are often embarrassed by this silly process, and in the interest of departmental peace, and also trying hard not to abuse their power, they rarely give anyone less than a good evaluation. A genuinely good evaluation therefore has to be expressed in superlatives that would tempt even Mahatma Gandhi into hubris.

Occasionally a supervisor will decide to ignore this pretty standardized corporate culture and actually write a legitimate evaluation of somebody. The supervisor's purpose may be noble, even self-sacrificing, doing this task strictly in the best long-term interest of the employee. In fact, this had better be the motivation of the supervisor, because he's not going to get anything else out of it except a headache.

Since the performance appraisal usually requires the signature of the guy being appraised, the supervisor is bound to get an argument. This isn't surprising. The supervisor has violated ordinary customs and practices at the company. In other words, the guy being evaluated feels he's been denied due process of the law. Suddenly this is a Fourteenth Amendment issue. As he righteously argues his case, he will be inwardly hearing the chorus of "The Battle Hymn of the Republic."

At this point, the supervisor had better be a good negotiator or the whole thing could explode to embarrassing proportions. After all, what does the guy getting a bum evaluation have to lose? He figures if he's going to be fired unjustly, why not try to publicly embarrass and humiliate the bastard who did it? If he's going to be booted out the door, maybe he can take the supervisor with him.

If the supervisor is to avoid the worst aspects of an ugly scene, he had better have a knack for negotiating. Howard Raiffa, a professor at the Harvard Business School, has adopted a study of thirty-two senior lending officers in major American banks who ranked thirty-four possible characteristics of negotiators. The list itself is interesting, and worth a look, but I wouldn't take the rankings too seriously. For one thing, a slight change in wording might have gotten a different ranking. This is often the case with survey data. For another thing, did these thirty-two senior loan officers know what they were talking about? You'd have to see the results of their loans. Maybe they had something to do with the loans to Poland, Mexico, Argentina, Brazil, and other countries teetering on the brink of default. In other words, these might be the same people who have nearly wrecked the entire international monetary system. Or maybe they were the people who lent money to the various domestic energy companies that went broke in the past couple of years. Finally, other professional negotiators, such as *you* negotiating your own raise, might rank the items differently.

In any case, here are the results in descending order:

1. Preparation and planning skills

2. Knowledge of subject matter being negotiated

3. Ability to think clearly and rapidly under pressure and uncertainty

4. Ability to express thoughts verbally

5. Listening skills

6. Judgment and general intelligence

7. Integrity

8. Ability to persuade others

9. Patience

10. Decisiveness

11. Ability to win respect and confidence of opponent

12. General problem-solving and analytical skills

13. Self-control, especially of emotions and their visibility

14. Insights into others' feelings

15. Persistence and determination

16. Ability to perceive and exploit available power to achieve objective

17. Insight into hidden needs and reactions of own and opponent's organization

18. Ability to lead and control members of own team or group

19. Previous negotiating experience

20. Personal sense of security

21. Open-mindedness (tolerance of other viewpoints)

22. Competitiveness (desire to compete and win)

23. Skill in communicating and coordinating various objectives within own organization

24. Debating ability (skill in parrying questions and answers across the table)

25. Willingness to risk being disliked

26. Ability to act out skillfully a variety of negotiating roles or postures

27. Status or rank in organization

28. Tolerance to ambiguity and uncertainty

29. Skill in communicating by signs, gestures, and silence (nonverbal language)

30. Compromising temperament

31. Attractive personality and sense of humor (degree to which people enjoy being with the person)

32. Trusting temperament

33. Willingness to take somewhat above-average business or career risks

34. Willingness to employ force, threat, or bluff to avoid being exploited

These were the rankings made by senior loan officers. What about a manager who decides to do an honest performance appraisal of a new guy on the job? What kind of effective negotiating characteristics would she need? A lot of good ones, you can be sure of that.

This was the situation in which Jill, twenty-nine and married, found herself. She is an officer at a huge Florida insurance company who supervises a staff of six. Among them is Tony, twenty-three and single. He thinks of himself, perhaps with some accuracy, as a stud, and he had been giving hot looks in Jill's direction for the ten months he had held the job. She had thought of simply telling him to cut it out, but she was worried about a public scene. A couple of times in the past, on hot days, she had worn some sexy outfits to work and got the disapproving look of her own boss. She wore the most conservative of business suits after that, but would still have felt better if she didn't do anything to raise the issue of her sexual appeal. So Jill simply gave Tony the cold shoulder. Unfortunately, this didn't cool Tony's ardor.

But her performance appraisal did. She has to write one annually for each member of her staff. She had until then given everyone a good report, and the good people spectacular ones, which is what virtually every other supervisor does. At this company, faint praise means one should report to work the next day, but tread lightly.

The catch in Jill's plan was that Tony had to sign the performance appraisal before it started to poison his personnel file. Naturally, when he saw what was written, he refused to sign. In fact, he screamed his head off.

Jill's performance appraisal focused on the three areas that she said needed improvement:

Written reports—"Sloppy and incompetent."

Verbal reports—"Poor . . . cocky style . . . condescending manner . . . shoots from the hip."

Attitude—"Leaves things for tomorrow . . . inability to deal with decision making . . . doesn't give a damn."

Everything she said in the appraisal was true, and she knew that Tony would be fired unless he shaped up. But because he was constantly coming on to her, she had felt very awkward about giving him proper supervision. She had two basic goals in this negotiation:

- The Official Goal: Get him to improve his work in each of the three areas.

- The Hidden Agenda: Get him to leave her alone.

She figured if she knocked him in line on the three topics mentioned in the performance appraisal, he'd cave in on the hidden agenda. Despite everything, she liked Tony and figured with the right direction, he'd work out.

Jill worked out her walkaway point by asking herself what she didn't want but was afraid she might get out of this negotiation. The answer was obvious: He would refuse to sign the appraisal. It would go to her boss and there might be an embarrassing confrontation. So she knew she'd have to concede something on the appraisal to quiet Tony down. The problem was that, as with most annual performance appraisals, she had no back-up data. She decided that the only thing she could prove was the section dealing with Tony's verbal reports. She had her boss, who had complained to her about it, as a witness. So she would stick with that and make whatever concessions she felt were necessary on the other points. She figured she was including the hidden agenda topic in her walkaway point merely by sticking to her guns on one of the other areas.

Corollary Twenty-five:

You can quickly establish a multi-issue walkaway point by looking at the overall situation for what you don't want but are afraid you might get. You can then look at each issue in turn to decide which issues are critical or which ones you can successfully defend.

(There is a fancier method in Game Theory to work out a walkaway point in a situation that involves negotiating over more than one issue. You can take each issue and assign it a weight as part of an overall walkaway package. I'll take up this topic in the next chapter.)

Jill looked over the list of bargaining characteristics contained in this chapter and decided that two were particularly relevant. She was going to be persistent and determined, and she was going to show a willingness to be disliked.

Tony fought her tooth and nail on each point, constantly pointing out that she had no specific facts to support her "wild and totally unfounded claims." He had her on this, and she knew it. She finally threw in the towel on the attitude section by telling him to write what he thought was appropriate. As for the section on written reports, she gave in a bit here, agreeing to say that he had started out poorly but had gotten a lot better in the course of the ten months. However, she stood fast on verbal reports. He said he would write his own section on verbal reports and append it to the report. He would point out how wrong he thought she was.

Jill had the final version retyped, and in fact even softened some of the language in the section on verbal reports. The net result was that the evaluation was hardly distinguishable from the usual innocuous performance appraisal. Tony signed without appending anything.

What about the hidden agenda? Tony hasn't given Jill a hot look since the day of the meeting, and his work has gotten a lot better, too. Jill told me she thought the performance evaluation was totally useless for its ostensible purpose, but great for communicating hidden agendas. Incidentally, she is planning to give Tony a very favorable performance appraisal next time.

There are several issues from Game Theory in this chapter:

- **Realize the basic rules of the game: An honest performance appraisal of a sloppy subordinate could put you, the supervisor, in an awkward position. This could be true for three reasons:**

  * You may have no back-up data to support your negative assessment.

  * You may be violating the corporate culture by taking the assessment seriously.

  * You may be open to charges of a hidden agenda.

- **There may be more than one issue under discussion in the performance appraisal. You can decide which are most critical to you and which you can throw away, and use this as a guide in working out your walkaway point. (Another way to work out a**

> **multi-issue walkaway point will be discussed in the next chapter.)**

- **Look over the list of bargaining characteristics in this chapter and see which ones you think you should be aware of for your negotiations.**

50

Negotiating for a New Job

BIG SHOTS ALWAYS BARGAIN over the terms of their jobs. A new CEO will negotiate salary, bonuses, stock options, his exit pay if things don't work out—the so-called golden parachute—and even the mortgage on a suitable house. The fact that someone bargains over all of these points can be used as a reliable guide for spotting big shots: *A big shot is somebody who always turns down the first offer.* At the middle management level this concept is also true.

For example Elise, thirty-four, was an assistant vice president at a major Florida accounting firm. She worked in an extremely specialized field—investment counseling for the idle, filthy rich—in other words, international playboys with palaces in Italy, châteaus on the Loire, and estates in Palm Beach.

Although her job performance was exceptional, her salary was low—her annual salary wouldn't cover the monthly restaurant, liquor, and cocaine bills of most of her clients. However, Elise had an exceptionally good reputation at several other firms, and there was a shortage of such talent in the industry. In fact, only six months earlier, one of her colleagues had been hired out by a major New York firm. Shortly after he took the new job, top management at the New York firm interviewed

Elise. They offered her a $9000 increase, which would have brought her salary up to a competitive level. The rest of the offered job was the same as her present one. She turned the job down because it was too similar to what she already had.

But she did tell her own boss, as well as his boss, about the offer. Her boss's boss subsequently gave her a dozen roses, a note of contrition for her low salary, and a raise to match the offer she had turned down. From a Game Theory point of view this is interesting. She wasn't threatening anything directly, since she had already turned down the other job offer. But her firm quickly moved to eliminate potential future threats by raising her salary to competitive levels.

However, her immediate boss felt embarrassed, since he was the one who had allowed her salary to fall dangerously low. He decided to end his embarrassment by trying to get rid of Elise. He did this by hiring a new V.P. who would become Elise's immediate boss. Elise should have gotten the post. Outraged, she was about to phone the New York firm when it beat her to it. They decided she was a big shot and made her a big offer. Her title would be vice president and she would answer only to her conscience and the head of the division in New York. Her salary would be $55,000—not bad for someone who had been making $34,000 only a few months earlier.

She was tempted to accept, but as a courtesy first informed her firm of what was going on. Notice what is happening here. Her walkaway point of moving up to market salary has been left in the dust. The New York firm has given her a new walkaway point.

Corollary Twenty-six:

If you are being auctioned off, and the bids already exceed your original walkaway point, your new walkaway point is simply the highest bid.

But the auction wasn't over for Elise. Her Florida firm matched the offer of the New York one in every detail plus a kicker—she could expand her territory to include both North America and Mediterranean Europe. She's still at her old firm.

Elise's job negotiation is obviously not the ordinary one, especially for the kid who's new on the block. When you're getting your first job in an industry, you obviously can't negotiate the details, right? Wrong.

You can negotiate because:

1. Individuals in both line and personnel have invested some time, perhaps a fair amount, in a search for the best candidate, and then in deciding that you're it. To a small degree, you have them entrapped, where they are willing to invest a little more time to listen to you, and almost certainly will not take back the offer they have already made. They have too much energy and time invested in putting that offer together.

2. They believe that you are the best person they can find for the opening or else they wouldn't have made the offer. If you politely reject the offer by asking for a bit more, they will not be offended. They'll think that you consider yourself a potential big shot.

3. They have probably offered you less than their walk-away point. This is so that a small fry in personnel can look bigger in the eyes of his boss.

4. Because the job is low-level, you will likely be negotiating not with your line boss but with personnel. So you are unlikely to ruffle the feathers of the guy to whom you will be reporting. If he hears from personnel that you are negotiating for a bit more, he will probably be amused and respect you a bit more.

5. Besides salary, the other issues that you negotiate will probably not be critical in their eyes.

6. You may catch personnel off balance, because they probably aren't used to haggling with someone at the

bottom of the heap. This can only work to your advantage.

Corollary Twenty-seven:

You can negotiate even low-level job offers. The company will almost never withdraw its last job offer—they are very slightly trapped by it.

The whole issue is how to work out your multi-issue walkaway point, which I'll call a walkaway package. A method for doing so was briefly described in the previous chapter, which dealt with negotiating a performance appraisal. An example may be helpful.

Roger, twenty-four, had worked at a large manufacturing company for two years. Suddenly he was given notice that his entire division was being closed out within the next three months. He started looking around for another job the same day. He had been in the marketing section of his department and had come in contact with the TV networks that carried his company's ads. He went to one of his contacts and asked about job possibilities. Four months and five lengthy interviews later, by which time Roger was unemployed, the personnel office of the network asked what kind of salary he was looking for.

He decided to add a couple of items to salary:

- Tuition payment for an MBA he would like to start. If the network would pick up this tab, it would be worth about 25 percent of the whole decision.

- A vacation right away, since he had missed his because of the layoff, worth about 5 percent of the whole decision.

Salary was therefore worth 70 percent of his decision. Naturally, a different person might look at different factors or weight the same ones differently. For example, here's how someone in the computer industry weighted the factors for his job change:

- Money, worth about 50 percent of the decision

- How much future he saw in the company, worth about 25 percent of the decision

- Pension and medical benefits, worth about 5 percent of the decision

- Where the job is—travel time—worth about 20 percent of the decision.

A woman in advertising, offered a job in North Africa, used only three criteria in her evaluation:

- Money, worth about 35 percent of the whole decision

- Housing, servant, and car allowance, worth about 25 percent of the whole decision

- Attributes of the job, worth about 40 percent of the whole decision.

You might have other criteria. In working out a walkaway package, it doesn't matter how many or what they are, providing the weights add up to 100 percent. This matters a great deal. You should try to categorize each of the different issues so they are independent of each other. That way you're not inadvertently giving anything an extra weight by counting it more than once.

Getting back to Roger, he had to decide how to establish his walkaway package. He decided that the salary factor, worth 70 percent, could be evaluated as follows: The absolute maximum he figured he could get was $22,000, and $17,000 was the least he thought they might offer. He could rate these amounts on a

scale of 5 for the top figure of $22,000 and 0 for the bottom fig-
ure of $17,000. Then he could multiply each of these scale
values by his salary weighting factor of 70 percent. The result
would be the salary score for each offer:

$22,000   This has a scale value of 5, which is multiplied by
           the salary factor weight of .7 to equal a salary
           score of 3.5.
$21,000   This has a scale value of 4, which is multiplied by
           the salary factor weight of .7 to equal a salary
           score of 2.8.
$20,000   This has a scale value of 3, which is multiplied by
           the salary factor weight of .7 to equal a salary
           score of 2.1.
$19,000   This has a scale value of 2, which is multiplied by
           the salary factor weight of .7 to equal a salary
           score of 1.4.
$18,000   This has a scale value of 1, which is multiplied by
           the salary factor weight of .7 to equal a salary
           score of .7.
$17,000   This has a scale value of 0, which is multiplied by
           the salary factor weight of .7 to equal a salary
           score of 0.

Next, Roger figured that the network would either pay all,
some, or none of the tuition for his proposed MBA. He rated
these on a scale of zero through five:

Pay all   This has a scale value of 5, multiplied by
            the tuition weight factor of .25 to equal a
            tuition score of 1.25.
Pay some   This has a scale value of 2.5, multiplied by
            the tuition weight factor of .25 to equal a
            tuition score of .625.
Pay none   This has a scale value of 0, multiplied by
            the tuition weight factor of .25 to equal a
            tuition score of 0.

Finally, there was the issue of the early vacation. If he gets it, he scores it at 5; if he doesn't, he scores it at 0:

He gets it.

This has a scale value of 5, multiplied by the vacation weight factor of .05 to equal a vacation score of .25.

He doesn't get it.

This has a scale value of 0, multiplied by the vacation weight factor of .05 to equal a vacation score of 0.

Notice that different issues can be evaluated by this method:

- All or nothing: the vacation issue.

- Only a few possible values: the tuition tab issue.

- A continuous range: the salary issue.

Roger figured out his walkaway package. He didn't have a job, but he had some savings and could hold out for a while. His last job had payed him $18,000, so he set his walkaway package at simply getting a pay offer of $18,000, with none of the other benefits. This gave him a score of .7 for salary plus nothing for anything else. Pretty lousy, but he was unemployed.

He asked for:

- $22,000, which has a salary score of 3.5

- Full tuition, which has a tuition score of 1.25

- A vacation right away, which has a vacation score of .25.

To get the total score of his package, add up the separate scores for each component: 3.5 + 1.25 + .25 = 5. He went for the works. The network replied with an offer of $19,000, partial tuition, no early vacation. The total score of their reply: 1.4 + .625 + 0 = 2.025. This wasn't a great offer, but was already higher than Roger's walkaway package. Roger very politely rejected it, asking for $21,000, full tuition, and an early vacation. He was going for a total score of $2.8 + 1.25 + .25 = 4.3$.

The network replied with an offer of $19,500 and agreed to pay full tuition if he got all A's, otherwise they'd pay only partial tuition. They also agreed to let him take one week of his vacation early. None of the values of this package actually fit the numbers in Roger's calculations, but he conservatively estimated it to be worth about $1.75 + .625 + .125 = 2.5$. They had come up from a total score of 2.025, not a substantial increase but an increase nonetheless. Roger grabbed the offer. He found out later that both the personnel director and his line V.P. offered him the extra $500, the scheme for full tuition, and half his vacation early because they were amused by his negotiation. Roger's negotiation paid off. He slightly increased his situation and started out with added respect at the network.

Roger told me that the key to the whole negotiation was working out his walkaway package, and once the give-and-take began, realizing he was negotiating entirely above it. He got a kick out of the whole business, because he wasn't acting out of desperation.

This chapter contains several lessons from Game Theory:

- **If you are lucky enough to be the object of a job-bidding war, your walkaway package is simply the highest bid.**

- **You can negotiate even low-level job offers. If done politely, the act of negotiating will almost certainly not cancel a first offer from the company.**

- **You can compute a multi-issue, weighted walkaway package.**

Part 8
Conclusion

51

You Don't Need a Mentor

IF YOU CAN ASK somebody you trust what to do, and he or she gives good advice, what do you need Game Theory for? You don't. Let your mentor solve your problems. Why rack your own brain? Just hope your mentor stays healthy, doesn't move out of town, and always has time for you.

There are several different kinds of mentors, the first of which is the Park Bench Mentor. In other words, he's not an active participant in the corporate battles. Why does he advise you? The best way to find out is to ask him. Often the mentor will see you as a member of his clan, broadly, even sentimentally defined. Ethnic, religious, racial, or sexual communality is often the key here. The mentor may see himself in you five, ten, or twenty years earlier.

But if he is in the fray himself, he's either in your faction or a rival one. If it's a rival one, be careful. Why is he advising you? He's double-crossing somebody and using you to do it. Are you sure that you are being used to your advantage?

Finding your own personal Deep Throat Mentor might be very useful for a specific game, but will it last to the league playoffs? It did for Woodward and Bernstein in their exposé of the Watergate scandal. But that had a clear end. In other words, once the facts were out, end of story. Congress got into the act, leaving Woodward and Bernstein to try to live happily ever after with their well-deserved fame and fortune. Most situations described in this book don't fit that kind of pattern. They are smaller incidents which form part of a story that could run for thirty or forty years. You could be in a jam and wait in the underground parking garage for your Deep Throat Mentor, but he may not turn up. This could create a problem if you've developed a dependency on him.

This leaves a mentor in your own faction. The first question to ask is, why is he so nice to you? There are a number of possibilities, including:

- He's a great guy.

- He likes you.

- His interest in you is primarily sexual.

- He's been assigned to you as mentor by his boss. Believe it or not, some companies assign new arrivals the person who is supposed to be their most loyal confidant, harebrained as this may seem.

- You could be useful to him.

If he's a great guy, or he likes you, terrific. You may have hit pay dirt. If his interest is chiefly sexual, you'll have to work out how to break the news, whatever the news might be. If he's been assigned to you, neither of you has much choice in the matter—although you both may be able to tacitly and by mutual consent ignore the whole embarrassing business. But if you're useful to him, the question again is why? This is a critically important question because it brings up the issue of the fall guy.

Sydney Greenstreet played the mentor to Elijah Cooke, Jr., in *The Maltese Falcon*. At a key point in the plot, Greenstreet, to save his own skin, turns Cooke into the fall guy. But this sort of thing happens only in the movies. Or does it? John Mitchell was the original mentor to John Dean in the Nixon White House. We now know that Dean was being set up to be a fall guy. Often, junior clumpers are expected to prove themselves by doing dirty jobs for which they will take the rap if the dirt is exposed. The protégé might be able to survive without the mentor, but the reverse may not be the case. Hence Corollary Twenty-eight:

In any organization where misdeeds are discovered,

there is only one person who is always indispensable—the fall guy.

For the proof of this, apply the Basic Decision-making Principle of Game Theory: If the mentor doesn't have a fall guy but needs one, what is it that he doesn't want but is afraid he might get? The rap. If the mentor does have a fall guy, what is it he doesn't want but is afraid he might get? Trouble finding a new protégé.

Office sharks are another kind of mentor to watch out for. Take a look at the sharks in your office. Most of them probably don't have mentors because office sharks often try to eat their mentors. We looked at an example of this in Chapter 24. However, some sharks are accompanied by bit players, analogous to pilot fish. The lesser lights aren't going anywhere on their own unless the shark goes, too. In fact, this is exactly what happens. The shark gets promoted and the pilot fish go along for the ride, getting their own smaller promotions. We may mistakenly think that the Shark Mentor is looking after the little nobodies. He does put up with them and occasionally socializes with them on an off day. But they remain, in the shark's eyes, little wimps who pose no threat to him. For proof of this, see how the shark refers to the small fry when they're not around. The pilot fish, however, unwisely believe that the shark is their mentor. This is unwise because the Shark Mentor will never give advice that could make his followers a threat to him. Sharks are not that stupid. For this reason, office sharks are notoriously lousy teachers, and the pilot fish will remain forever dwarfed by their traveling companions. A good mentor, on the other hand, sees his pupils as his protégés and encourages them. They don't have to wait until their mentor swims off into retirement in the Bermuda Triangle before they can really get ahead.

The Game Theory of this is interesting. As I said earlier, sharks don't use Game Theory but act instead out of pure intuition. However, we can use Game Theory to model a Shark Mentor's thinking: "If I teach this little parasite everything I know, what is it I don't want but am afraid I might get? Bitten in the jugular vein. If I keep him in my wake, what is it I don't want but am afraid I might get? A pest." Which would the Shark Mentor choose if he thought about it? But he doesn't have to think about it.

Sometimes the prospective mentor is a decent guy who has your best interests at heart, is not trying to use you to cover up his shenanigans, and is not trying to keep you permanently in his shadow. But he does have a significant flaw—he gives bum advice. The Bumbling Mentor is in some ways the most dangerous, because in your position of inexperience, you don't know his advice is lousy. As we have seen, looking at how successful he is by no means is a sure guide to the value of his counsel. He may simply be an amiable and lucky clumper who was favored along with a lot of other people because of some long-forgotten success. He was on the right side at the right time. The problem is doubly serious because of the nature of the mentor/protégé relationship. It isn't exactly one of pure equality, but is more akin to that of parent/child, where you play the kid. He's supposed to have the brains and you supply the energy and enthusiasm. For the relationship to continue, you have to act on his advice. This might be okay if you always know the score moment by moment. But as we've seen in a number of examples, you may not know the final consequences of an action until months later. But this man is giving you advice now and he may not have a brain in his head.

How can you test it to see if his pointers are any good? You can't. That's the whole problem. He's speaking to you in confidence, so you can't check it out with fellow clumpers. That would be indiscretion. Keep in mind also that your peers may be envious of your relationship with the mentor. Because of this you couldn't depend on the accuracy of their comments anyway. And you don't dare reveal what he said to outsiders. That would be treason.

Any time an elder member of the faction tacitly or explicitly offers to be your mentor, keep in mind one thing: Unless your mentor has been foisted on you by corporate bigwigs, you don't have to take any mentor who comes along. You can evaluate your relationship with a possible mentor and decide if he's the right one for you. How do you evaluate a possible mentor? Use the Basic Decision-making Principle of Game Theory: If I latch on to this prospective mentor, what is it that I don't want but am afraid I might get? Then ask the same question for the choice of not linking up with this guy. You might find that you're better off without him.

How does this fit in with factions? Recall our Thirteenth Corollary:

The middle manager loner will always fail.

This doesn't mean you need a mentor. It means you have to be in a faction—nothing more. A lot of very successful persons don't have mentors for reasons we have just examined. They belong to a faction, but they don't have a mentor.

Notice that in the more than fifty cases in this book, a mentor played no role. From this we arrive at Corollary Twenty-nine:

You don't need a mentor.

If you can find a good one, great, but if you can't, don't let it worry you. You won't be on your own. You'll be in a faction and you'll be better off being your own counselor. Some of the most successful persons are, and you could be one of them. But although you are your own counselor, you won't be left to your own devices. You'll have Game Theory—the Basic Principle and all of the corollaries. And as we've seen, that knowledge can turn a loss into a win.

Bibliography

Robert L. Banks and Steven C. Wheelwright, "Operations vs. Strategy: Trading Tomorrow for Today," *Harvard Business Review,* May–June 1979.

Robert Bell, *Having it Your Way—The Strategy of Settling Everyday Conflicts.* New York: W. W. Norton, 1977.

Robert Bell and John Coplans, *Decisions, Decisions—Game Theory and You.* New York: W. W. Norton, 1976.

Robert H. Hayes and William J. Abernathy, "Managing Our Way to Economic Decline," *Harvard Business Review,* July–August 1980.

Steve J. Heims, *John von Neumann and Norbert Weiner—From Mathematics to the Technologies of Life and Death.* Cambridge, Mass.: MIT Press, 1980.

Percy H. Hill, et al., *Making Decisions.* Reading, Mass.: Addision-Wesley, 1979.

Chester B. Karrass, *Give and Take.* New York: T. Y. Crowell, 1974.

Hope Lampert, *Till Death Do Us Part—Bendix vs. Martin Marietta.* New York: Harcourt Brace Jovanovich, 1983.

R. Duncan Luce and Howard Raiffa, *Games and Decisions.* New York: John Wiley, 1957.

John McDonald, *The Game of Business.* Garden City, N.Y.: Doubleday, 1975.

Oskar Morgenstern, "The Collaboration Between Oskar Morgenstern and John von Neumann on the Theory of Games," *Journal of Economic Literature,* September 1976.

John von Neumann and Oskar Morgenstern, *The Theory of*

Game and Economic Behavior. New York: John Wiley, Science Editions (paperback), 1964.

Gerard I. Nierenberg, *The Art of Negotiating.* New York: Cornerstone Library (paperback), 1968.

Michael E. Porter, *Competitive Strategy—Techniques for Analyzing Industries and Competitors.* New York: The Free Press, 1980.

Howard Raiffa, *The Art and Science of Negotiation.* Cambridge, Mass.: Harvard University Press, 1982.

Anatol Rapoport, *Two-Person Game Theory—The Essential Ideas.* Ann Arbor: University of Michigan Press, 1966.

——, *N-Person Game Theory.* Ann Arbor: University of Michigan Press, 1970.

Thomas L. Saaty, *Mathematical Models of Arms Control and Disarmament.* New York: John Wiley, 1968.

Thomas Schelling, *The Strategy of Conflict.* New York: Oxford University Press, 1960; Galaxy Book, 1963.

Index

Office sharks
  as mentors, 245–246
  outmaneuvering, 149–154
Order
  achieving prominence with, 146
Over-kindness
  of boss, 31–33

Pay raises, 144
  in negotiating for a new job,
    233–240
  standard formulas for, 196–201,
    205–209, 215–219
Peers. *See* Colleagues
Performance appraisals, 225–233
Perquisites
  faction membership and, 188–189
  in negotiating for a new job,
    233–240
Personnel
  dueling over, 71–75
Place
  achieving prominence with, 145
Poker, 59
Political persons
  countering strategy of, 129–133
Politics
  fanatics on, 154–157
Price
  achieving prominence with, 146
Principle, 93–100
Prisoner's Dilemma, 106–109
Productivity, 5
Prominence
  muscling by, 143–149
Promotions
  advantages of, for bosses,
    202–203
  arguments of bosses against,
    201–202
  asking for, 34–38

without outside job offer,
    37–38
  with outside job offer, 35–37
  deal-making in, 203–204,
    207–209
  Horatio Alger myth and, 12–13
  intimidation tactics and, 25–26
  of office sharks, 245
  overspecialized careers and,
    211–212
  of secretaries, 12–13, 43–45
  standard formula for, 196–201,
    205–209, 215–219
Psychotherapy, 177

Race
  achieving prominence with,
    147
  factions based on, 182
Raiffa, Howard, 227
Relatives of important people,
    84–88
Religion
  achieving prominence with, 147
Respect, 11
Responsibility
  for information about rival firms,
    164–167
  for mistakes, 51–55
Retrenchments, 88–92

Salary
  in overspecialized career,
    210–215
  in negotiation for a new job,
    233–240
Sales incentives, 59–65, 151–153
Salespeople
  fanatics and, 154–155